Charles Hosmer Walcott

Concord in the colonial Period

Being a History of the Town of Concord, Massachusetts

Charles Hosmer Walcott

Concord in the colonial Period
Being a History of the Town of Concord, Massachusetts

ISBN/EAN: 9783337154301

Printed in Europe, USA, Canada, Australia, Japan

Cover: Foto ©ninafisch / pixelio.de

More available books at **www.hansebooks.com**

CONCORD

IN

THE COLONIAL PERIOD

Being a History

OF THE

TOWN OF CONCORD, MASSACHUSETTS

FROM THE EARLIEST SETTLEMENT TO THE OVERTHROW OF THE
ANDROS GOVERNMENT

1635—1689

By CHARLES H. WALCOTT

WITH MAP

BOSTON
ESTES AND LAURIAT
1884

University Press:
JOHN WILSON AND SON, CAMBRIDGE.

TO

THE PEOPLE OF CONCORD

This Study of the Early Times

IS RESPECTFULLY DEDICATED

BY THE AUTHOR.

"My desire is that no mans Spectacles may deceive him, so as to look upon these things either as bigger or lesser, better or worser, then they are; which all men generally are apt to doe at things at so great distance, but that they may judge of them as indeed they are, by what truth they see here exprest in the things themselves."

THOMAS SHEPARD.

PREFACE.

THIS volume is the result of the labor of many months spent in exploring the original sources of our town's early history, — researches made in the belief that a re-examination of the authorities, conducted in the modern spirit of historical inquiry, would develop new and interesting facts, and enable us to realize more fully the stern but conscientious self-denial, persevering industry, and sturdy good sense that actuated the settlers of this town.

Constant reference has been had to Shattuck's History of Concord, which was published almost fifty years ago, and has been a valuable aid in the prosecution of the studies which led to the preparation of this book.

If the statements and inferences herein contained do not always agree with those of the earlier work, the reader may be assured that the difference is not due to neglect of the considerations which led Mr. Shattuck to the results stated by him, but is more especially to be attributed to the greater facility with which records and documents may now be consulted, in consequence of the great amount of money, labor, and thought, that have been devoted of late to arranging, copying, printing, and indexing early writings of a historical character; so that the close application and thought, once largely exhausted in deciphering old records and private documents, may now, in many instances, be used to extract the full meaning of what is written, and to determine its exact relations to information obtained from other sources.

In almost every instance, Mr. Shattuck's authorities have been consulted anew by the author of this volume; and some additional sources of information have been drawn upon, which the elder writer seems not to have discovered.

The extracts and ancient documents here printed have been carefully compared with the originals whenever the latter could be found, but it will appear that, in a few instances, the author has been unable to find original papers to which Mr. Shattuck undoubtedly had access. Two documents are for this reason reprinted from his history, without being verified by the present author. Extracts from the Records of the Colony (cited under their printed title of "Massachusetts Records") are taken from the printed volumes.

To avoid confusion, it should be borne in mind that all dates before 1752 are according to the old style, which made the year begin on the 25th day of March. The months, beginning with March, were alluded to, as also were the days of the week, by numbers, instead of by names. Thus, April 20, 1640, would be indicated as $20^{th} : 2^d : 40$, or $20^{th} \ 2^{mo} \ 1640$. In writing dates occurring between January 1st and March 25th, sometimes the double date is given; but, otherwise, it is to be understood that the later year, beginning in January, is retained. For instance, March 12, $169\frac{5}{6}$ may be found written, March 12, 1696; and 8th 12mo 1664 would appear as February 8, 1665.

Of the two oldest record books of the town, which together, as copied by Mr. David Pulsifer, are now comprised in Volume I. of the "Ancient Records of Concord," the earlier, — which, in all probability, was procured in 1653, soon after the division of the town into Quarters, — contains records of grants and divisions of land, voted by the company of the South Quarter. There are also brief lists, descriptive of the first-division lands, and, to a limited extent, the second-division lands, owned by dwellers in the South (or West) Quarter. Written at the top of a page is the following declaration of the purpose for which the book was intended: —

"The Records of this booke of the weast quartter one the south syde of the mill brooke, concernes second devisions as upland, second devisione meadow, & woodland, acordinge to mens seuerall pportions & alowances that is due to them, aproved & alowed off, by the wholle company as is expresed in the severall pages followinge."

This old book also contains records of ways laid out in the South Quarter, rates made to defray the expenses of building bridges and highways, and accounts of the labor done or furnished in furtherance of these public works. The latest date is 1724.

It cannot be doubted that there once was a town book, which contained the records of the earliest grants of land, and, probably, the other proceedings of the inhabitants, meeting together in general assembly. A book of this character is referred to in ancient deeds and other documents, as well as in the records that remain to us, and is designated as "the old towne booke of Concord," or the "town's register booke."

This volume was extant in 1664, when it was decided to have a new book, and to copy into it "what is in the old booke, that is vesefull." The "new book" then obtained is in the office of the town clerk, and forms the second half of the first volume of "Ancient Records," as copied. It contains, under date of "5. of 12 : m? 1635," (February 5, 1636), the entry concerning the location of the meeting-house, which, of course, was copied from something earlier. This book contains records of grants of lands and the laying out of ways, beginning with 1653 and extending to 1804. There are, also, a few deeds, leases, and agreements concerning the division or fencing of lands, and a few of the East Quarter records are here preserved.

These early books of the town's records have been constantly referred to and studied in the preparation of this work. They are not expressly cited, except in a few instances, because it was thought better to allude generally, once for all, to an authority which, if referred to in every instance, would appear on almost every page of this book.

It has been deemed wise to present the thoughts and acts of the men who lived in the times here treated of, to a considerable extent in their own language; and, with this in mind, many extracts from original records and documents have been included, in the printing of which the utmost care has been exercised to reproduce the original as closely as possible. These extracts should be read without regard to spelling or punctuation, both of which, judged by our standards, are as bad as they could well be; but these are only slight obstructions, after all, to one who carefully seeks for the meaning of what is written.

The subject is in its nature local, and the larger history of the colony has been treated of only when it was found to be closely connected with that of the town, or when reference to it was deemed necessary for a more complete understanding of the position and relations of the town and its people to the world without. The author cannot flatter himself with the expectation that his work will be found free from errors, or that, in weighing men and events of two centuries and a half ago, his readers will always take the same point of view, or draw the same inferences, as are here presented. Earnest efforts have been made to present the facts accurately, to distinguish between knowledge and inferences, — in short, to present the subject in the light of truth, without exaggeration or suppression of any facts of public interest.

CONCORD, April, 1884.

LIST OF AUTHORITIES CITED.

Acts and Resolves, Public and Private, of the Province of the Massachusetts-Bay.

Billerica Town Records.

Bond's (Henry) Genealogies and History of Watertown.

Butler's (Caleb) History of Groton, Mass.

Concord Town Records.

Drake's (Samuel A.) History of Middlesex County.

Emerson's (Ralph W.) Historical Discourse in 1835.

Foster's (Edmund) Littleton Century Sermon. 1815.

Gookin's (Daniel) Historical Account of the Doings and Sufferings of the Christian Indians. Reprinted in vol. ii. 423-534, of the Transactions and Collections of the American Antiquarian Society.

Hazen's (Henry A.) History of Billerica, Mass.

Hotten's Lists of Emigrants to America.

Hubbard's (William) Narrative of the Indian Wars in New England, 1677.

Hutchinson's (Thomas) History of Massachusetts, 1628-1750.

Johnson's (Edward) Wonderworking Providence of Sion's Saviour in New England, 1654. Reprinted in the Collections of the Massachusetts Historical Society, 2d series, ii. 49, *et seq.*

Lechford's (Thomas) Plain Dealing: or Newes from New England, 1642. Reprinted in the Collections of the Massachusetts Historical Society, 3d series, vol. iii.

Liberties of the Massachusetts Colony in New England, The, 1641. Reprinted in the Collections of the Massachusetts Historical Society, 3d series, viii. 191-237.

Manuscript Records of the General Court preserved in the State Archives.
Massachusetts Records.
Mather's (Cotton) Magnalia Christi Americana, 1702.
Memorial History of Boston.
Middlesex County Court, Records and Files.
Middlesex Records of Deeds.
Palfrey's (John G.) History of New England.
Ripley's (Ezra) Half-century Sermon, 1828.
Savage's (James) Genealogical Dictionary of New England.
———— Gleanings for New England History. Printed in the Collections of the Massachusetts Historical Society, 3d Series, viii. 243, et seq.
Sewall's (Samuel) Diary. Printed in the Collections of the Massachusetts Historical Society, 5th series, vol. v.
Shattuck's (Lemuel) History of Concord, Mass., 1835.
Shattuck's (Lemuel) Papers preserved in the Library of the New England Historic Genealogical Society.
Shepard's (Thomas) Cleare Sunshine of the Gospell, 1648. Reprinted in the Collections of the Massachusetts Historical Society, 3d series, v. 25-67.
Suffolk Probate Records.
Suffolk Records of Deeds.
Wheeler's (Thomas) Narrative of an Expedition with Capt. Edward Hutchinson into the Nipmuck Country, and to Quabaog, now Brookfield, Mass., 1675. Reprinted in New Hampshire Historical Collections, ii. 5.
Winthrop's (John) History of New England from 1630 to 1649 (Savage's ed.), 1853.

TABLE OF CONTENTS.

                                                      PAGE

LIST OF AUTHORITIES CITED xi

CHAPTER I.

The Planters and the Plantation. — Map of the Original Grant and Blood's Farms. — Purchase from the Indians. — First Meeting-house. — The Church. — Town Officers. — Case of Ambrose Martin. — John Hoar and Philip Read 1

CHAPTER II.

Early Trials. — Withdrawal of Mr. Jones. — Loss of the Leaders. — Rev. Peter Bulkeley, Simon Willard, Thomas Flint. — The Kentish Influence 33

CHAPTER III.

The New Grant, or "Concord Village." — Blood's Farms . 49

CHAPTER IV.

The Second Division of Lands. — Division of the Township into Quarters. — Roads and Bridges. — Bulkeley's Farm. — Flint's Farm. — Other Large Allotments. — Undivided Lands. — Land Transcripts. — Location of House-lots. — Peter Bulkeley, Esquire. — Second Meeting-house. — Town Pound. — Mills. — Burying-Grounds 67

CHAPTER V.

PAGE

Relations with the Indians. — King Philip's War. — Fight at Brookfield. — Nashoba Indians. — Constable John Heywood's Return 100

CHAPTER VI.

The Militia. — Education. — Charities. — Mining and Manufactures. — Public Houses. — Amusements, &c. — Freemen. — The Andros Revolution 120

INDEX 155

CONCORD

IN

THE COLONIAL PERIOD.

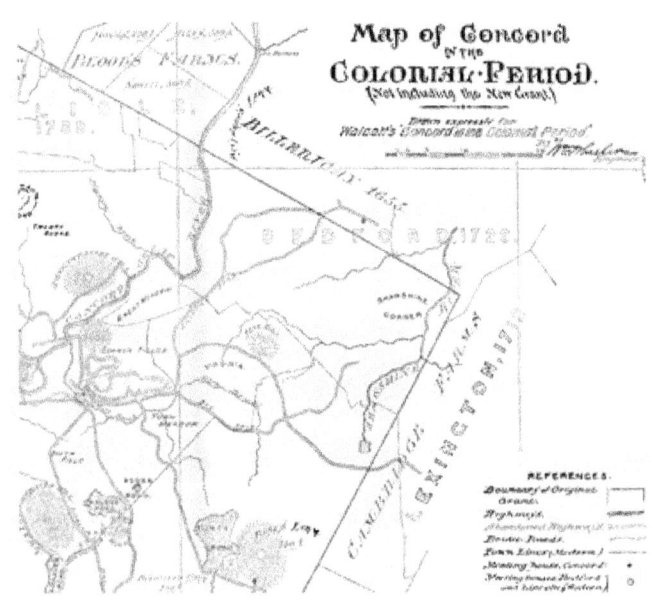

CONCORD IN THE COLONIAL PERIOD.

CHAPTER I.

"Beneath low hills, in the broad interval
Through which at will our Indian rivulet
Winds mindful still of sannup and of squaw,
Whose pipe and arrow oft the plough unburies, —
Here in pine houses built of new-fallen trees,
Supplanters of the tribe, the farmers dwell."

EMERSON.

THE PLANTERS AND THE PLANTATION. — MAP OF THE ORIGINAL GRANT AND BLOOD'S FARMS. — PURCHASE FROM THE INDIANS. — FIRST MEETING-HOUSE. — THE CHURCH. — CASE OF AMBROSE MARTIN.

THE plantation at Musketaquid was settled by Rev. Peter Bulkeley, of Odell in England, associated with Simon Willard, a merchant, of Horsmonden, who brought with them about twelve families.

Mr. Bulkeley, then fifty-two years of age, embarked at London, May 9, 1635, in the ship "Susan and Ellen," accompanied by William Buttrick and Thomas Brooke. Mrs. Bulkeley sailed two days before, in the "Elizabeth and Ann," under the escort of Thomas Dane;[1] from which it may be inferred that

[1] Savage's "Gleanings;" Hotten, pp. 76, 77.

by the temporary separation of husband and wife, the orders prohibiting the departure of clergymen and "subsidy men" were more easily evaded.[1]

James Hosmer was provided with a certificate from the minister of Hawkhurst, in Kent, and the attestation of two justices of the peace that he and his family were "conformable to the Church of England," and were "no subsidy men."[2] Both Mr. Bulkeley and Thomas Flint had sufficient property to bring them within the degree of "subsidy men," and therefore it may be supposed that their departure was achieved by obtaining a special license, or through the connivance of the authorities; but the rest of the Concord company were plain people, of humble station in England, and of small means, who hoped in the New World to better their condition, and to enjoy unmolested the simpler forms of religious worship that their tastes and consciences approved.

There was, however, no transplanting of a church and its pastor, — like the removal of John Robinson and his flock to Holland, or like the settlements at Plymouth and Dorchester. Few, and possibly none, of Mr. Bulkeley's parishioners, except his own family,

---

[1] The order of the Lords Commissioners for the Colonies, passed in December, 1634, forbade the emigration of all persons of the degree of a "subsidy man" without a special license, and of all persons beneath that degree without evidence of their having taken the oaths of supremacy and allegiance, and of their conformity to the orders of discipline of the Church of England. Palfrey, i. 396.

[2] Hotten, p. 53.

followed him across the sea; and there is no reason to suppose that the Concord settlers ever came together on English soil. The church was not gathered until the summer following the actual settlement of the town, nor was its organization completed until the ordination of the elders in the spring of 1637. The homes of the pioneers were, moreover, widely separated. Mr. Bulkeley lived in Bedfordshire; Simon Willard, James Hosmer, and probably William Buss and Thomas Dane, were from Kent; John Heald came from Berwick in Northumberland; William Hunt and Jonathan Mitchell had their homes in Yorkshire; William Buttrick came from Kingston-on-Thames, in Surrey; Derbyshire was represented by Thomas Flint, and probably William Wood. It is not unlikely that other parts of England supplied their contingents to the little band who, after many struggles and with the aid of a compass, succeeded in pushing through the wilderness that then bounded Watertown on the northwest, and arrived at their new home in the fall of 1635.

The following extracts from Johnson's work, written ten or fifteen years later, are interesting, although coming from a writer whose imagination sometimes lends too strong a coloring to his facts: —

"Upon some inquiry of the Indians, who lived to the North West of the Bay, one Captaine Simon Willard, being acquainted with them by reason of his trade, became a chiefe instrument in erecting this towne. The land they purchase of the Indians; and with much difficulties travelling through unknowne woods, and through watery swamps, they discover the fitnesse of the place, — sometimes passing through the thickets, where their hands are forced to make way for their bodies passage, and their feete clambering over the crossed trees, which when they missed they sunke into an uncertaine bottome in water, and wade up to their knees, tumbling sometimes higher and sometimes lower. Wearied with this toile, they at end of this meete with a scorching plaine; yet not so plaine but that the ragged bushes scratch their legs fouly, even to wearing their stockings to their bare skin in two or three hours. If they be not otherwise well defended with bootes or buskings, their flesh will be torne, that some being forced to passe on without further provision, have had the bloud trickle downe at every step; and in time of summer the sun casts such a reflecting heate from the sweet ferne, whose scent is very strong, so that some herewith have beene very nere fainting, although very able bodies to undergoe much travell, and this not to be indured for one day, but for many; and verily did not the Lord incourage their natural parts (with hopes of a new and strange discovery, expecting every houre to see some rare sight never seen before), they were never able to hold out and breake through. . . .

"Their further hardship is to travell sometimes they know not whether, bewildred indeed without sight of sun; their compasse miscarrying in crowding through the bushes, they sadly search up and down for a known way, the Indian paths being not above one foot broad, so that a man may travell many dayes and never find one. . . .

"This intricate worke no whit daunted these resolved servants of Christ to go on with the worke in hand; but lying in the open aire, while the watery clouds poure down all the night season, and sometimes the driving snow dissolving on their backs, they keep their wet cloathes warme with a continued fire, till the renewed morning give fresh opportunity of further travell."

Their destination was the "six miles of land square" granted them by the General Court, and to be laid out at the place called by the Indians

"Musketaquid," but thenceforth to be known as Concord. On Sept. 2, 1635, the General Court passed the following order.[1]

"It is ordered, that there shalbe a plantacōn att Musketequid, & that there shalbe 6 myles of land square to belong to it, & that the inhabitants thereof shall have three yeares immunities from all publ[ic] charges, except traineings ; Further, that when any that plant there shall have occacōn of carryeing of goods thither, they shall repaire to two of the nexte magistrates where the teames are, whoe shall have power for a yeare to presse draughts, att reasonable rates, to be payde by the owners of the goods, to transport their goods thither att seasonable tymes ; & the name of the place is changed, & here after to be called Concord."[2]

There is no plan of the original grant, if, indeed, such a plan was ever made; nor is there any return of the laying out of the land, such as was usually prepared and filed. We do, however, know that it was in fact laid out, and bounds set at the corners, and without doubt this work was done by Simon Willard.

The author is not aware that any one has before attempted to construct a map of Concord as it was in the beginning. The map published with this work is the result of a comparison of maps, plans, and old records, supplemented by observations made on the

---

[1] Mass. Records, i. 157.

[2] In March following it was further "agreed, that the immunitie of Concord for three yeares shall begin the first of October nexte, & that none shall have benefitt thereof but those that lyve there, & with respect onely to the stocke they have there." Mass. Records, i. 167. The order authorizing the impressment of carts was renewed Oct. 28, 1636, for a year longer. — *Ibid.*, 182.

ground. It has been carefully drawn, under the author's direction, by Mr. William Wheeler of Concord, whose assistance has been invaluable in the application of tests which lie peculiarly within the province of a skilful surveyor and draughtsman.

Briefly, the sources of information which assist us in constructing a map like this are the following : —

Two plans by Jonathan Danforth, dated, respectively, 1660[1] and 1706,[2] show Billerica land on both sides of the Concord River, and are valuable for our purpose as showing the south line of Billerica, which was identical with the north line of Concord, except where they bounded on Blood's Farms.

A plan of Bedford made in 1760 and in the library of the Massachusetts Historical Society shows the Billerica line east of the river.

Among the Shattuck papers is a somewhat dilapidated plan of Concord Village, which, possibly, is the plan alluded to by Mr. Shattuck[3] as having been made by Captain Stephen Hosmer in 1730. This gives us the western boundary of the original grant, throughout its entire length.

In the State archives is a collection of plans of the several towns in the Commonwealth made in response to a resolve of the General Court passed in 1794, and another more elaborate set made under similar authority in 1830. Concord in 1795 is shown

[1] In the library of the Mass. Historical Society.
[2] Mass. Archives, Ancient Plans, v. i. p. 191.
[3] History, p. 280.

by a plan drawn from actual surveys by Ephraim Wood. The town lines were then the same as at present. The survey of 1830 was made by John G. Hales, and resulted in a well-drawn map, copies of which were sold with Shattuck's History of Concord, published five years afterwards. H. F. Walling's map of the town was made in 1852, and his map of Middlesex County in 1856.

The lines, courses, distances, and angles shown by this multitude of maps and plans have been carefully studied and compared in the preparation of the map here presented.

The original grant was laid out in the form of a square. Right angles and straight lines were preferred by the early settlers whenever they could be had. No other grants had been made near this place; consequently it was not deemed necessary to notify any adjoining owner of the running of the line, and the simplest possible form was adopted.

The original grant may be bounded as follows: Beginning at the southwest corner at a stone post which marks the present southwest corner of the town, the line runs north 40° east (approximate needle course) on the Acton line to a stone at the present northwest corner of Concord, near the Dudley place. When Acton was made a town, the statute [1] bounded it on the east by "Concord old bounds;" from which it appears that Acton includes no part of the original Concord, and that the dividing line be-

[1] July 3, 1735. See Prov. Laws, ii. 763.

tween the two towns is a portion of the old Concord line on that side. The Acton boundary extended leads to a heap of lichen-covered boulders surmounted by a stake. This ancient monument is near the top of a hill in the southwesterly part of Carlisle, and undoubtedly marks the old northwest corner of our town. It was identified and pointed out to the writer on the ground by Major B. F. Heald, of Carlisle, who says that he has often heard his father and other ancient men, long since deceased, speak of this bound as marking the old Concord corner; and everything goes to corroborate this testimony. The place was commonly known by the name of "Berry Corner," and was the original northeast corner of Acton; but, in 1780,[1] a portion of that town near this point was included in what was then constituted as the District of Carlisle, and subsequently formed a part of the town of the same name.[2]

Making a right angle at this corner the line runs southeasterly through the lower part of Carlisle, coinciding in two places with our present boundary, and, crossing the river, runs about a quarter of a mile to the southward of the main street of Bedford and parallel with it, to a point on the upland about forty rods east of the Shawshine River. Ancient stone walls preserve this line in part. The bound at the northeast corner must have been removed at some

[1] Statute passed April 28, 1780.
[2] Carlisle did not acquire all the legal characteristics of a town until February 18, 1805. 3 Special Laws, 497.

time after Bedford was incorporated; and, as it stood in cultivated land, near a house, the farmer would not be likely to value it so highly as we should, had he allowed it to remain. The corner can be located with sufficient accuracy however, by the intersection of the north line, just described, with the line on the east; and it appears from the Billerica records of 1700 that the corner was then marked by a stake and stones.[1]

[1] The following is taken from the town records of Billerica, where it appears under the date of Feb. 11, 1699–1700. " by agreement betwene the Town of Concord & Billerika the bounds betwene these Towns were renued & whereas severall of the old bounds were rotten and lost they now agreed to make new bounds instead thereof or instead of them. We began at Concord South east Corner, which was a stake & stones about it standing on the South east of Shawshin River about fourty poles from it & kept the old bound trees untill we came at the great Cedar Swamp, & through the sd swamp (all though the trees in it were marked sum what Crooked) yet we renued the old marks, untill we came within six score pole of Concord River unto a great white oake very often & old marked and betwene this white oake & the River there being no more bounds to be found. we agreed to Run from this white oak unto sd River upon a point Running North fivety & three degrees west & marked the bounds sufficiently which line did cut cross Abraham Tailors a little before we came at the River this is a tru draft of what is concluded relating unto the premises as attest

"JONATHAN DANFORTH

" *Surveier.*"

This renewal of the bounds was assented to by Joseph French, Samuel Davis, Jr., and Thomas Brown, the Concord committee, and by Davis, French, and Abraham Taylor, as proprietors of lands adjacent to the line. As reasons for doing the work at this time it was urged that the season was favorable, " because of passing the swamps upon the yice & it had not bene thoroughly don for sum years."

This agreement, with some verbal discrepancies, which do not alter the sense, is recorded at the end of the second volume of the Concord

Returning to the southwest corner, we run southeasterly on the present Sudbury line to the river, and thence in the same course, on the Wayland line, to the corner at Lincoln; then striking across the lower corner of Lincoln and keeping in the same straight line, we come to a heap of stones situated near a brook, and in a line with that part of the boundary between Lincoln and Weston which extends southwesterly from the great road at G. F. Harrington's house. Turning and making a right angle at this corner, we proceed towards the northeast, on old stone walls, just touching the eastern edge of Beaver Pond and including a portion of the boundary between Bedford and Lexington,[1] thus meeting our north line and completing the square.

The reader will naturally expect to find the sides of the square measuring just six miles each, but

records, but, as some words are worn off at the edges of the leaves, it was thought best to follow the records of Billerica.

[1] The southerly bounds of Bedford ran eastward by a crooked line "to Lexington bounds, and keeping Lexington line to Billerica line, to a stake and heap of stones, *being the northeasterly corner of Concord*; from thence continuing on Lexington line to a stake and heap of stones called Woburn Corner, &c." St. 1729; Prov. Laws, ii. 527.

The bounds by which Lincoln was set off in 1754, ran northward from the Boston road "to Bedford line; and by Bedford line to Concord Corner, adjoining to Lexington, &c." The "Corner" here referred to was, of course, the new corner made when Bedford was set off, as distinguished from the old Shawshin Corner mentioned above; and the statute above cited, taken with the statute defining the Bedford bounds, establishes beyond a doubt that the present northeast corner of Lincoln was in the old Concord line.

they are found, in fact, to measure almost exactly six and two-thirds miles. On Hosmer's plan, before referred to, the length of the western boundary is given as six miles and one hundred and forty-two rods. In the present state of our information the length of these lines cannot be stated with exactness, because of difference in the results shown by recorded surveys. The discrepancies, however, do not affect the conclusions already reached by us, and are not so surprising when the length of the lines is considered, the nature of the ground to be traversed, and the fact that no such accuracy was needed or desired as would be considered necessary in the measurement of smaller tracts bounded by shorter lines. The writer is informed that, in locating land grants in Pennsylvania, it has been customary to add ten per cent as an allowance for poor land; and it appears from papers in our own State archives that, in locating other grants in Massachusetts in the early times, it was permissible to add something to the amount granted, "for rocks and waste land." Moreover, it is well known that the early grants as laid out almost always exceeded the amount named in the grant. Some of the excess in our case may have been allowed for public roads, and part, no doubt, was for slack in the chain.

Annexed to every grant of land by the General Court was the condition, either expressed or implied, that no prior grants should be interfered with. Probably the thought never entered Willard's mind that this restriction would cause any difficulty in fixing the bounds of his rectangular township in the wild woods of Musketaquid; for Concord was the first settlement above tide-water, and when he had set his bounds, he believed them to be surrounded on every hand by unappropriated wilderness. It was claimed, however, by the Watertown men that the lines of their grant, running eight miles into the country, converged to a point north of Walden Pond, thus seriously marring the mathematical simplicity of Willard's plan. An appeal to the Court resulted in an order, August 20, 1638, that Watertown lines should extend so far only "as Concord bounds give leave."

The tract of wilderness land thus enclosed was occupied, in a sense, by two or three hundred Indians, who eked out a miserable existence by hunting and fishing, with the help of such planting and reaping as was compatible with their slothful ignorance and imperfect tools fashioned of wood and stone, clam shells and bones of animals.

As early as 1636, at the house of Rev. Mr. Bulkeley, a treaty was made with the Indians, by the terms of which the entire tract, six miles square, was ceded to the English "undertakers." The following depositions taken in 1684, are interesting evidence of this interview. They are recorded in the town records, as well as with Middlesex Deeds, but where the copies differ, those in the county records are preferred as having been made from the originals.

"The Testimony of Richard Rice aged seventy-two years Sheweth that about the yeare one thousand six hundred Thirty six there was an Agreement made by some undertakers for the Towne since called Concord[1] with some Indians that had right unto the land then purchased for the Township The indians names was Squaw Sachem, Tohuttawun Sagamore, Muttunkatucka, and some other indians y^t lived then at that place, The Tract of land being six miles square, The center of the place being about the place the meeting house standeth now, The bargaine was made & confirmed between ye English undertakers & the Indians then present, to their good sattisfaction on all hands.

"7 . 8 . 84.   Sworne in Court

"Tho Danforth Record^r"
[Middlesex Deeds, Lib. 9, fol. 105.]

"The Testimony of William Buttrick aged sixty-eight years or thereabouts Sheweth, That about the yeare one thousand six hundred thirty & six, there was an Agreement made by some undertakers for the Towne since called Concord with some Indians that had right unto the land then purchased of them for the Towneship; the Indians names was Squaw Sachem Tohuttawun Sagamore & Nuttankatucka & some other Indians that lived and was then present at that place & at that time. The Tract of land being six miles square, The center being about ye place the meeting house now standeth on. The bargaine was made & confirmed between the English undertakers & the Indians then present & concerud, to theyr good sattisfaction on all hands

"7, 8, 84.   Sworne in Court

"Tho: Danforth. R."
[Middlesex Deeds, Lib. 9, fol. 105.]

"The Deposition Jehojakin alias Mantatucket a christian Indian of Natick aged. 70 years or thereabouts,

---

[1] This expression, which also appears in Buttrick's testimony, taken alone might convey the impression that the name *Concord* was applied subsequently to 1636; but the order of the court authorizing the plantation affixes the name. *Ante*, p. 5.

"This Deponent testifyeth & sayth, that about 50 years since he lived within the bounds of that place which is now called Concord at the foot of an hill named Nawshawtick now in the possession of Mr Henery Woodis & that he was p^{r}sent at a bargaine made at the house of Mr Peter Bulkly (now Capt Timothy Wheeler's) between Mr Simon Willard Mr John Jones, Mr Spencer & severall others in behalfe of the Englishmen who were setling upon the s^d Towne of Concord & Squaw Sachem, Tahuttawun & Nimrod Indians which s^d Indians (according to y^r particular Rights & Interests) then sold a Tract of land conteyning six mile square (the s^d house being accounted about the center) to the s^d English for a place to settle a Towne in. And he the s^d Deponent saw s^d Willard & Spencer pay a parcell of wompompeag, Hatchets, Hows, Knives, Cotton Cloath & Shirts to the s^d Indians for the s^d Tract of land: And in p^{r}ticular he the s^d Deponent perfectly remembreth that Wompachowet Husband to Squaw-Sachem received a Suit of cotton cloath, an Hatt, a white linnen band, shoes, stockins & a great coat upon account of s^d bargaine And in the conclusion the s^d Indians declard themselvs sattisfyed & told the Englishmen they were Welcome. There were also present at the s^d Bargain Waban, Merch^t Thomas his brother in law Nowtoquatuckquaw an Indian, Aantonuish now called Jethro

"taken upon oath. 20th of October 1684

"Before Daniel Gookin Senr. Asisis^t

"Tho: DANFORTH. Dep^t. Govr."

[Middlesex Deeds, Lib. 9, fol. 100.]

"The Deposition of Jethro a Christian Indian of Natick aged 70 years or therabouts

"this Deponent testifyeth & sayth, That about 50 years since he dwelt at Nashobah, near unto the place now named by the English Concord & that coming to s^d Concord was p^{r}sent at the making a bargaine (which was done at the house of Mr Peter Bulkly w^c now Capt. Timothy Wheeler liveth in) between severall Englishmen (in behalfe of such as were setling s^d place) viz: Mr Simon Willard, Mr John Jones, Mr Spencer & others on the one party And Squaw Sachem, Tohattowan & Nimrod Indians on the other party: And that the s^d Indians according to y^r severall rights) did then sell unto the s^d Englishmen a certeyn Tract of land conteyning six miles square (the s^d house being accounted about ye center) to plant a Town in. And that he the s^d Deponent did see the s^d Willard & Spencer[1] pay to the s^d Indians for the s^d Tract of land a parcell of Wompompeag, Hatchetts, Hows, Knives Cotton Cloath & shirts & that Wappacowet Husband to Squaw Sachem had of the s^d English upon the Account of the s^d bargain, a new suit of cotton cloath, a linnen band, a hat, shoes, stockins and a great Coat, & y^t after the s^d Bargaine was concluded Mr Simon Willard, poynting to the four quarters of the world declared that they had bought three miles from that place east west, north & south & the s^d Indians manifested their free consent thereunto. there were p^{r}ent at the making of the s^d Bargaine amongst other Indians, Waban, Merch^t, Thomas, his Brother in law Notawquatuckquaw & Jehojakin who is yet living & dposeth in like manner as above.

"7 . 8 . 84 Sworne in Court by Jethro.
"Attests THO: DANFORTH. R."
[Middlesex Deeds, Lib. 9, fol. 106.]

Judged from our point of view, the price was insignificant, but the Indians seem to have been satisfied, and it is probable that the main purpose and

---

[1] William Spencer, who was present when the bargain was made with the Indians, and received grants of land in this neighborhood, was a prominent citizen of Cambridge and a magistrate. The name of Spencer Brook is a pleasant reminder of one whose interest in Concord was contemporary with the birth of the town.

In 1654, Samuel Adams, of Charlestown, conveyed to Richard Temple, of the same town, " the land in Concord that was sometimes Mr Wm Spencer's" (Middlesex Deeds, L. 1, f. 129); but there is no reason to suppose that Mr. Spencer was ever a resident here. The land was a large tract on both sides of the road, at Angier's Mills.

value of the treaty of purchase consisted in the establishment of friendly relations with the occupants of the soil. The colonists preferred the derivation of their title through the royal charter and the grant of the General Court, but were not averse to strengthening their position by any suitable means that were offered.

We find that, May 17, 1637,—

"Concord had leave graunted them to purchase the ground wthin their limits of the Indeans, to wit, Atawans & Squa Sachim."[1]

The following record appears under date of August 1, 1637:—

"Webb Cowet, Squaw Sachem, Tahatawants, Natan quaticke alias Oldmans, Caato, alias Goodmans[2] did expresse their consent to the sale of the weire at Concord over against the towne & all the planting ground wch hath bene formerly planted by the Indians, to the inhabitants of Concord, of wch there was a writeing, wth their marks subscribed given into the Court, expressing the price given."[3]

Whether the transaction of which this record and "writeing" were the evidence related to the original grant and the agreement entered into in Mr. Bulkeley's house, or to something not included in those negotiations, is not clear.

It is a curious fact that Jethro and Jehoiakin say

---

[1] Mass. Records, i. 196.

[2] Sudbury (five miles square) was bought of this "Caato, alias Goodmans." He had a wigwam on a hill near the centre of Sudbury, still known as Goodman's Hill. Drake's Middlesex, ii. 358.

[3] Mass. Records, i. 196.

that Mr. Bulkeley's house was "accounted about the center," while Buttrick and Rice fix the central point at "about the place the meeting house standeth now."[1] This discrepancy seems to indicate that the township was not laid out with reference to any object as the exact centre, but with a view solely to practical advantages and resources. Willard, who had previously traded with the Indians in this neighborhood, knew what the country was, and so laid out his bounds as to include six valuable mill sites, seven natural ponds, more than nine miles of river, and a large number of smaller streams. The meadows traversed by the sluggish rivers that ran by devious windings to the northward, were bordered by tracts of upland that had been burned over and brought under rude cultivation by the natives, and afforded a large area of cleared land that was very attractive to the English settlers. The woodland was for the most part covered with pine. Shad, salmon, and alewives abounded in the rivers and brooks, which were also the haunts of fur-bearing animals. Willard was specially interested in the fur trade, and it is likely that this tract, so abundantly supplied with ponds and water courses, was selected and laid out with particular regard to the prosecution of that business.[2]

[1] *Ante*, pp. 13, 14.
[2] In 1641 a company was formed, with Simon Willard at the head of it, and endowed with a monopoly of the trade with the Indians, of which the traffic in beaver skins formed a very considerable part. Mass. Records, i. 322, 323.

The first dwelling-places were under the ridge of land that extends in an easterly direction from the Town House, and was known in early days as "the hills." Immediately upon the arrival of the first settlers, according to Johnson,

> "they burrow themselves in the earth for their first shelter under some hill-side, casting the earth aloft upon timber, they make a smoaky fire against the earth at the highest side. . . . In these poor wigwams they sing psalmes, pray and praise their God, till they can provide them houses, which ordinarily was not wont to be with many till the earth, by the Lord's blessing, brought forth bread to feed them, their wives and little ones, which with sore labours they attain."

As soon as the most pressing needs of the situation were met, allotments of land were made to the members of the company, and house-lots were laid out with some regularity on both sides of the Mill Brook, eastward as far as the Kettle place lately owned by Mr. Staples, and on Walden Street to the Almshouse; in a westerly direction as far as the Damon place; and to the Old Manse and the Edmund Hosmer place on the north. Besides his house-lot, each one received his due proportion of planting-ground and meadow lying in the near vicinity. This was the first division of lands, the price paid into the common stock being a shilling per acre, or, in some special cases, a sixpence per acre. The land thus divided constituted a small part only of the whole grant, and the remainder was held in common and undivided, subject to such regulations as the inhabitants thought fit to establish, until the second division in 1653, by which, substantially, the whole remaining portion of the original grant was disposed of.

The civil affairs of "the company of the whole town" were managed by selectmen or "townsmen," who received formal instructions for their guidance from a committee chosen in town-meeting for that purpose. The instructions of 1672 are preserved in the town records.[1] The constable was an important

[1] "Instructiones given to the Selectmen of Concord for the year, 1672.

1. To see that the ministers Rates be discharged acording to time
2. To acsamen whether the meting house, be fiuised acording to agreement, & if not, that it may be; but if the agreement be fulfiled, then to take cear that somthing be done to keep the water out, and that the pulpet be altred
3. That ceare be taken of the bookes of marters & other bookes, that belong to the Towne, that they be kept from abeuce uesage, & not to be lent to any person more then one month at one time,
4. That spedy kere be taken to mend or demales, the foote bridg over the north Riv^r at the Iron Works;
5. To treat with Capt. Thomas Wheler about his leese of the Townes farme & if it may be upon Resonable termes to alter that perticuler wherein the Towne is Jn Jnioyned to send such a nomber cattle yearly to be herded by him ;
6. To let out the land & housing where now John Law dweles; for the benifet of the towne,
7. To take order that all Corne filds be sufficently fenced in seson, the Crane fild & bricke keld field especially;
8. And that incorigment be given for the destroing of blackeburds & Jaies;
9. That spesiall cear be taken to preuent damiag by swine in corne fieldes & medows
10. That shepe & lames be keept from doing damiag in cornefields;
11. To make a Record of all the habitationes, that are priviledged with liberty at Comones;
12. To take account of the laste yeares selectmen for what is don, [due?] to the Towne by Reent by John Law, or by givft by

personage elected by the town, but sworn in by the officers of the colonial government.[1] The selectmen were the agents and representatives of the town for almost every purpose, except appearing at the annual Court of Election, to which the town sent two deputies, who, under the colonial regime, were not required to be inhabitants of the town.[2]

It seems that in the older towns on the sea-coast, the selectmen were at first invested with limited judicial powers;[3] but, as early as 1638, it was ordered that commissioners " for ending of small matters," should be appointed for each town by the County Court, with jurisdiction of cases in which the debt or damage did not exceed twenty shillings.[4]

In 1639 the towns were ordered to keep records

    Joseph Meriam; or otherwise of wright dew to the Towne, not to Restraine the selectmen from lenity towards John Law;

13 To see that menes lauds both Improved & unimproved be truly broth. [brought in]

14 To take care that vndesiarable persones be not entertained; so as to become inhabitants

15 To take cere that psones doe not ouer Charg ther Comones with Cattle,

16 That all psones that have taken the oath of fidellity be Recorded,

17 That cere be taken that Cattle be herded, as much as may be, with convenence

    These perticolers were agreed upon by vs whose names are vnderwriten nchamia. hunt; John flint; John miles; Witt dated 4: 1. mo. $\frac{1631}{1632}$ heartwell; Thō: Wheler Joshuah brooke Joseph; heaward; Gershom. Brooke, Humpry barit John Billings "

    [1] Mass. Records, i. 248.

    [2] This was changed in 1693, the representative from Concord voting against the change.

    [3] Hutchinson, i. 398.

    [4] Mass. Records, i. 239.

of births, marriages, and deaths occurring within their respective limits. The officer to whom this duty fell was called "clerk of the writs," and later, "town clerk."

For the greater security of new settlements, the law prohibited the building of dwelling-houses (except mill-houses and farm-houses of such as had their dwelling-houses in some town) more than half a mile from the meeting-house, unless by the consent of the court.[1] This order was at first observed, but as the town increased in population, new houses were built on the more remote lands without regard to the prohibition.

The first houses were humble structures, with thatched roofs, and, very likely, wooden chimneys. Oiled paper served in place of window glass. Hastily constructed of perishable materials, not one of these buildings remains. They were replaced before the lapse of many years by houses of a more substantial character, generally facing the south, with shingled roofs running almost to the ground on the back, brick chimneys, and a projecting second story. Some of the second set of houses were dignified with the name of "mansion," but none has survived to furnish us with a specimen of the architecture favored by the second generation.

By its first recorded vote the town decided, Feb. 5, 1636, that the meeting-house — temple of church and state — should "stand on the hill neare the

[1] Mass. Records, i. 157.

brooke on the east side of goodman Judsons lott."[1]
Nothing in the town or county records affords any
light on the location of this lot, but the testimony
afforded by tradition has pointed with little vari-
ation to the top of the hill in or near the old burying
ground, as the site of the first meeting-house. The
meeting-house at Dedham, built about the same time,
was thirty-six feet long, twenty feet wide, and twelve
feet high " in the stud." It was thatched with long
grass, and was probably not unlike the house built
by our ancestors. Long before the second building
was erected on the Common (substantially where the
Meeting-house of the First Parish now stands), there
was a lot of land in the east part of the town known
as " the meeting-house frame ; " and, unless this odd
name can be accounted for in some better way, it
may be thought to indicate the land which supplied
the timber for the first place of public worship.[2]

The Church of Concord was formally gathered at
Cambridge, July 5, 1636, being, in point of time,
the thirteenth church organized in the colony; and

---

[1] William Judson came to America in 1634, and settled in Concord the following year with his wife, Grace, and sons, Joseph, Jeremiah, and Joshua. All removed in 1639 to Hartford, but were residents of Stratford in 1644, where the sons remained; but the father and mother went to New Haven, where she died Sept. 29, 1659. Savage's Genealogical Dictionary.

[2] This lot is referred to in the town records of lands in 1666, as " the place caled the meting house frame." June 20, 1694, Francis Fletcher conveys to his son Joseph *inter alia*, ten acres in the easterly part of the town, called " ye Meeting House fframe, upon which the old Saw mill stands." Middlesex Deeds, L. 13, f. 409.

the organization was completed April 6, 1637, when Rev. Peter Bulkeley was chosen teacher, and Rev. John Jones, pastor.[1] The latter, a graduate of Oxford University, arrived in October, 1635,[2] and joined the Concord company. There was, at this time, a distinction between the office and duties of teacher and those of pastor, but none of the authorities state the difference clearly. The terms soon became convertible, and the functions of both offices were discharged by one person.

Governor Vane and Deputy-Governor Winthrop were invited to be present at the gathering of the church, but, on account of a real or fancied breach of etiquette, failed to attend.[3] Fine-spun theories about "legal preachers" and the effect of ordination by the bishop in England kept from the ceremonies of ordination the governor, and Rev. John Cotton, Mr. Wheelwright, "and the two ruling elders of Boston, and the rest of that church which were of any note did none of them come to this meeting."[4] This matter is worth mentioning only as showing that the Concord ministers received no encouragement

[1] Winthrop, i. 114, 225, 259.
[2] Winthrop, i. 202.
[3] "Mr Buckly and Mr. Jones, two English ministers, appointed this day to gather a church at Newtown, to settle at Concord. They sent word, three days before, to the governour and deputy, to desire their presence; but they took it in ill part, and thought not fit to go because they had not come to them before, (as they ought to have done, and as others had done before) to acquaint them with their purpose." Winthrop, i. 225.
[4] Winthrop, i. 260.

at the beginning of their undertaking from those of whom they would have been most likely to expect it, and from whom a word of cheer would have been most welcome. However, it mattered little, for they had fixed their habitations in the wilds and must, sooner or later, content themselves with their own resources. After the departure of Mr. Jones, in 1644, Mr. Bulkeley was sole pastor, at a salary of £70,[1] until his death in 1659. Lechford speaks of the "catechizing of children" and others, as a practice peculiar to the Concord Church; and Mather says of the pastor,[2] "he was very laborious, and because he was, through some infirmities of body, not so able to visit his flock, and instruct them from house to house, he added unto his other publick labours, on the Lord's days, that of constant catechizing; wherein, after all the unmarried people had answered, all the people of the whole assembly were edified, by his expositions and applications."

Edward Bulkeley, who had been for some years minister at Marshfield, succeeded his father, with a salary of £80; but as he was no longer young, and was afflicted with lameness, it was soon deemed expedient to procure the services of a colleague, and accordingly in 1667, Rev. Joseph Estabrook, born in Enfield, England, and educated at Harvard College, was engaged at a salary equal to Mr. Bulkeley's, to be paid half in money and half in produce.[3] The town voted, February 3, 1680, —

[1] Shattuck, 152.   [2] Magnalia, iii. c. 10.   [3] Shattuck, 161.

"That every house holder that hath a teame greate[r] or lesser shall accordingly cary yearly one loade of wood to the ministe[r] and every other house holder or rateable person to cut wood one day and for the ministers: and that the wood is to be equaly devided to too ministers as the selectmen for the time being shall appoynt."

Mr. Edward Bulkeley's pastorate ended, practically, March 5, 1694, when the town voted as follows: —

"Whereas their Rever^d Pastor M^r. Edward Bulkely is under such Infermatyes of Body by Reason of great age that he is not capeable of Attending the worke of the ministry as in times past, being Also sensible of the obligation that they are under to Afford to him a comfortable maintenance dureing the Terme of his natural life, that thereby they may Testefy their Gratatude for his former service in the Gospell, That they the sayd People of sayd Concord do hereby oblige ye sayd Towne to pay to ye s^d m^r Bulkely or to his certain order yearly & each year dureing his natural life, the sum of thirty pounds of mony the one halfe at or before the first of octob^r sixteen hundred ninty & four, & the otherer halfe at or before the first of May sixteen hundred ninety & five, which sum as above shall be paid yearly & each year upon the sayd Termes. and which sum of Thirty pounds truly payd as above, shall be in lieu of the former sallary of eighty pounds which the said people were obliged to have payd yearly to him the sayd mr. Bulkley for his ministerial service."

Mr. Bulkeley agreed to this change in his relations to the townspeople, but with the proviso that he should be "left at liberty by this agreement whether to Preach or not to preach any more in Concord." He died at Chelmsford, January 2, 1696, at an advanced age, and was buried at Concord.[1]

All church matters were passed upon at the meet-

[1] Sewall.

ings of the inhabitants held in the meeting-house. But, in settling a minister, it was customary for the members of the church to act in the first instance as a distinct body, and when an agreement was arrived at, they referred the result to the people for ratification in town-meeting. The town organization existed quite as much for the support of divine worship as for the maintenance of roads and bridges. For an instance of the mingling of functions caused by this union of interests, witness the following extract from the records of the year 1678: —

"agreement between John Cotten of Concord and ye too Deacons and : : the Selecte men of Concord — viz — y^t ye said Deacons have exchanged the Towen Cowe for another Cowe of the said John Cottens ye said John Cotten to have ye Town Cowe to kill and to have ye vse of the said Cowe now exchanged for ye Terme of tow years from ye date hereof next ensueing

ROBERT MERIAM
LUKE POTTER
JOHN COTTON."

It was the practice to choose a committee "to seat the meeting-house," who, in the execution of this delicate duty, were expected to consider the age, wealth, and social or official importance of the worshipper.[1]

Very early in the history of the plantation Mr. Ambrose Martin of this town asserted his right to freedom of speech, but, like Mr. John Hoar and Dr.

---

[1] The committee chosen March 7, 168$^9_0$, consisted of Captain Timothy Wheeler, Deacon Potter, John Smedly, Senior, Cornet Woodis, and John Flint, who added to their number Peter Bulkeley, Esq.

Philip Read at a later date, he found that the free expression of opinion on certain subjects was an expensive luxury. Martin's case, which arose in 1639, and attracted much attention,[1] well illustrates the sternness (to use no harsher term) of the colonial government; but some good came of the severity in this case, for it produced a most valuable document written by Mr. Bulkeley and signed by him and his associate and thirteen members of the church.

Martin's offence was that, in argument, he applied an unsavory epithet to the church covenant, styled it "a humane invention," and said that "hee wondered at God's patience, feared it would end in the sharpe," and that "the ministers did dethrone Christ and set up themselves." He was sentenced to pay a fine of £10, and, what was probably quite as unpalatable, advised " to go to Mr. Mather to bee instructed by him." Upon the delinquent's refusal to comply

---

[1] The matter is alluded to by Winthrop and by Lechford, both of whom give Martin the title of " Mr." or " Master," which was not generally applied, as with us, but was restricted to those who by reason of wealth, social position or public service were ranked as gentlemen.

" Now and then a baronet made his home for a time in Boston, but otherwise the highest title was Mr. or Mrs., and this title was applied only to a few persons of unquestioned eminence. All ministers and their wives took the title, and the higher magistrates; but it was not given to deputies to the General Court as such. The great body of respectable citizens were dubbed Goodman and Goodwife, but officers of the church and of the militia were almost invariably called by the title of their rank or office. Below the grade of goodman and goodwife were still the servants, who had no prefix to their plain names." H. E. Scudder, in Mem. Hist. of Boston, vol. i. p. 487.

with these orders, his cow was taken and sold, and subsequently a levy was made upon his house and land.[1]

The petition of the church above referred to was presented upon his refusal to accept the portion of the property remaining after the legal demands were satisfied. The original is preserved among the Shattuck papers, and is in Mr. Bulkeley's handwriting.

"To the Honoured Court.
"The Petition of the church of Concord in behalfe of our brother Mr. Ambrose Martin.

"Your humble Petitioners doe intreate, that whereas some yeares agoe, our sayd brother Mr. Martin, was fined by the Court for some unadvised speeches uttered against the church covent, for wch he was fined ten pounds, and had to the value of £20 by distresse taken from him, of which £20, there is one halfe remayning in the hands of the Countrey to this day, wch ten pounds he cannot be p^{r}swaded to accept of, unlesse he may have the whole restored unto him, (wch we doe impute unto his infirmitye and weakness) We now considering the greate decay of his estate, and the necessityes (if not extremityes) wch the familye is come unto, we intreate (as was sayd) that this honoured Court would please to pitye his necessitous condition, and to remitt unto him the whole fine wch was layd upon him, without w^{ch}, he cannot be p^{r}swaded to receave the prt wch is due unto him. Wherein if this honoured Court shall please to grant this our petition, we shall be bound to prayse God for your tender compassion toward this our poore brother"

    PETER BULKELEY
    JOHN JONES
    RICHARD GRIFFIN
    SIMON WILLARD   JOSEPH WHEELLER
    ROBERT MERRIAM   THOMAS FOXE
    THOMAS WHEELER   WILLIAM BUSSE
    GEORGE WHEELER   HENRY FARWELL
    ROBERT FLETCHER   JAMES HOSMER
    LUKE POTTER   JOHN GRAVES.

[1] Mass. Records, i. 252. And see Winthrop and Lechford.

Such a petition was entitled to be considered in the spirit that dictated it, but the application found no pity in the breast of that iron man, John Endicott. The same hand that tore the cross from the English flag wrote these words on the face of the petition:

"The case appeares to the Magistrates to be now past helpe through his own obstinacye; but for the over plus upon sale of the distresse, he or his wife may have it, when they will call for it."

Jo: Endecott Govr"

Indorsements: "The 5^t of the 4th moneth — 1644
"The petitⁿ of Ambrose Martyn of Concord.
Ordered by the q^{rt^r} co^rt."

The records of the County Court assure us that the "overplus" was never called for.[1]

Compared with other writings of the time, the letter of the church is remarkably clear, almost elegant, in style, and in its tone well calculated to accomplish its purpose. More than this, it is in perfect accord with the more enlightened humanity of the present time, and shows conclusively that, at that early day, the virtues of a tolerant spirit and a forgiving charity were highly esteemed by the

---

[1] "Whereas it hath been declared to this court that there was in house and land at Concord to the vallue of twelve pounds left in the handes of Moses Wheat & Thomas ffox by Ambros Martin deceased, which hath remained in their handes about nine or ten yeares, It is ordered by this court that it shall be divided in mann^r following, viz: in an equall division between the wife of Saml Raint & Jno Rogers to be payd by the above named parties with addition of foure pounds for the forbearance." Records, June 20, 1654.

people of this town, whose "religion was sweetness and peace amidst toil and tears."[1]

The prosecutions of Mr. John Hoar and Dr. Philip Read occurred about thirty years after the trouble with Martin, at a time when the less amiable characteristics of Puritanism were more marked here as well as elsewhere. The cases are worthy of mention because these men were, respectively, the earliest representatives in Concord of the legal and medical professions,[2] and because their experiences serve to show us the high consideration in which the persons and office of the ministers were generally held. That the proceedings against these citizens, based in one instance upon mere idle words, and in the other upon an opinion expressed in the practice of his profession of healing, were calculated to give permanent strength to any class of men in a thoughtful community, may well be doubted; but the sincerity of the prosecutors cannot be questioned. They honestly believed that adverse criticism of men whom they looked upon as set apart in a peculiar manner for the performance of duties especially sacred, was, in effect, an attack upon religion itself, which was the corner-stone of the commonwealth. The fault was in their logic, not in their hearts.

Hoar was an eccentric lawyer, well known, and

[1] Emerson's Historical Discourse.
[2] William Buss and Jonathan Prescott were described by the addition "chirurgeon," the exact signification of which, as applied to them, is not known.

correspondingly disliked, by the authorities, as a man of independent thought and a facile tongue, which was continually making trouble for him. Whether he held any peculiar theological or doctrinal views, which in our day would be considered entitled to respectful consideration, or merely gave vent to feelings of irritation against those who were unfriendly to him, is uncertain; but his courage and kindness of heart were unquestionable, and, as will appear, he was preëminent among his fellows in public spirit.[1]

About 1667, Philip Read, who wrote himself "Physitian," married the daughter of Richard Rice, settled near his father-in-law at the easterly end of the town, and practised his profession in Concord, Cambridge, Watertown, and Sudbury. A flood of litigation descended upon him in 1670, because he expressed an unfavorable opinion of Mr. Edward Bulkeley's powers as a preacher, in comparison with Mr. Estabrook,[2] and for saying when called to attend

[1] For uttering complaints that justice was denied him in the courts, he was compelled, in 1665, to give a bond for his good behavior, and was "disabled to plead any cases but his oune in this jurisdiction." Mass. Records, iv. pt. ii. 292. In 1668, he was fined £10 for saying "at Ensigne Willm Busse his house that the Blessing which his Master Bulkely pronounced in dismissing the publique Assembly in the Meeting-house was no better than vane babling." Subsequently, on two occasions at least, he was summoned into court to answer "for neglecting the public worship of God on the Lord's days." County Court Files, 1668, 1675.

[2] He said that he could preach as well as Mr. Bulkeley, who was called by none but a company of blockheads who followed the plowtail, and was not worthy to carry Mr. Estabrook's books after him. It is amusing to see what trifles were thought to endanger the welfare of church and state.

a female patient, that he thought her illness was caused by standing too long during the ceremony of administering the Lord's Supper. When charged in court with these offences, he fearlessly asserted his right to be represented by counsel, but his application to that end was refused. He was fined £20, and for a time found it more agreeable to live elsewhere.

NOTE. *Old Bounds.* — A map contained in Bond's Genealogies and History of Watertown, shows what purports to be the southeastern corner of the Concord grant. Many reasons might be given to prove the inaccuracy of the map in this respect, but one will suffice. The old Garfield estate, now occupied by Francis A. Wheeler, and lying on the eastern and southern borders of Beaver Pond, in the town of Lincoln, was conveyed, in the year 1712, by Benjamin Garfield, of Watertown, to his son Thomas, of the same town. The land is described as being one hundred and twenty acres, situated in Watertown, and is bounded on the west "with the Line between Watertown and Concord." Middlesex Deeds, L. 16, f. 324. Eight years afterwards, Thomas bought of Nathaniel Ball, of Concord, sixteen acres of upland and swamp adjoining the farm, and bounded easterly upon Weston line [the old Watertown line], westerly and southerly upon the brook running from Beaver Pond, and northerly upon the pond. Ibid. L. 22, f. 386.

The map above referred to shows the eastern line of Concord at a considerable distance to the westward of Beaver Pond, instead of grazing its eastern border.

CHAPTER II.

> "A shepherd of mankind indeed,
> Who loved his charge, but never loved to lead;
> One whose meek flock the people joyed to be,
> Not lured by any cheat of birth,
> But by his clear-grained human worth,
> And brave old wisdom of sincerity."
>
> LOWELL.

EARLY TRIALS. — WITHDRAWAL OF MR. JONES. — LOSS OF THE LEADERS. — REV. PETER BULKELEY, SIMON WILLARD, THOMAS FLINT. — THE KENTISH INFLUENCE.

IT is impossible to over-estimate the trials and actual suffering that were endured by the pioneer families. The writings of Mr. Higginson and others, which were prepared here for publication in the old country, were calculated to invest the Englishman of that day with the notion that, in soil and natural resources generally, New England was something like what we understand California to be. Here, as elsewhere in the colony, a close grappling with the facts was followed by inevitable disappointment. The meadows were wet,[1] the soil was found to require hard labor

---

[1] The following order was passed September 8, 1636: —

"Whereas the inhabitants of Concord are purposed to abate the falls in the ryver upon wch their towne standeth, whearby they conceive such townes as shalbee hereafter planted above them vpon the said

to make and keep it productive, and it is written, that the people were "forced to cut their bread very thin for a long season."

It cannot be wondered at that some sickened and died by reason of the unaccustomed hardships and severity of the winter weather, while others lost all faith in the success of the enterprise, sold their estates for a little, and departed. The cattle died, wolves preyed upon the herds; homesickness and fear of an Indian attack increased the burden of their lives, so that it became well-nigh greater than they could bear.[1] Dissensions arose, at last,

---

ryver shall receive benefit by reason of their charge & labor, it is therefore ordered, that such towns or ffarmes as shalbee planted above them shall contribute to the inhabitants of Concord pportionable both to their charge & adventure, & according to the benefit that the said townes or ffarmes shall receive by the dreaning of their medows." Mass. Records, i. 178.

Again, on November 13th, 1644, commissioners were appointed by the General Court " to set some order which may conduce to the better impveing of the said medow & saveing and pserving of the hay there gotten eithr by draining the same, or otherwise, & to pportion the charges layd out about it as equally & iustly (only upon those that oweth the land) as they in their wisdomes shall see meete." *Ibid.*, ii. 89, 99.

A committee was appointed May 15, 1672 " in answer to inhabitants of Concord & Sudbury petition to prevent damage by overfloiug on ye meadowes."

[1] Winthrop (ii. 36) records the following incident under date of April 13, 1641: —

" Upon the Lord's day at Concord two children were left at home alone, one lying in a cradle, the other having burned a cloth, and fearing its mother should see it, thrust it into a hay-stack by the door, (the fire not being quite out) whereby the hay and house were burned and the child in the cradle before they came from the meeting."

that threatened the very existence of the plantation.

The difficulty, not to say impossibility, of supporting two ministers, was very soon felt, and Winthrop says,[1] that on July 28, 1642, —

> "Some of the elders went to Concord, being sent for by the church there to advise with them about the maintenance of their elders, &c. They found them wavering about removal, not finding their plantation answerable to their expectation, and the maintenance of two elders too heavy a burden for them. The elders' advice was that they should continue and wait upon God, and be helpful to their elders in labor and what they could, and all to be ordered by the deacons, (whose office had not formerly been improved this way amongst them,) and that the elders should be content with what means the church was able at present to afford them, and if either of them should be called to some other place, then to advise with other churches about removal."

Glowing accounts, received from those who had gone farther westward, of better things to be attained in the Connecticut valley, served to increase the prevailing uneasiness, and in 1644, ere ten years had passed over the little settlement, Mr. Jones removed to Fairfield, on Long Island Sound, with about one eighth of the entire population. The persons whose names follow are either known or supposed to have accompanied Mr. Jones: Thomas Doggett, John Evarts, Jonathan Mitchell, William Odell, John Barron, John Tompkins, Benjamin Turney, Joseph Middlebrook, James Bennett, William Coslin (or Costin), Ephraim Wheeler, and Thomas Wheeler.

[1] History, ii. 88.

We are left in the dark as to the merits of the controversy that led to this secession, and it is as well so.[1]

Whatever may have been the immediate cause for the removal of Mr. Jones and his friends, it is certain that the defection was a misfortune from which Concord found it hard to recover. The separation was, however, inevitable, and in the end, doubtless, beneficial; for, in 1635, the proportion of the number of clergymen in Massachusetts to the entire population, was greater than in any other age or country of which we have any knowledge. They were, almost without exception, men of high character, education, and talents; but the difficulty lay in the fact that they were non-producers in a community where the paramount and ever pressing question was, how to produce the necessaries of life in sufficient quantity to supply the daily wants of the family. No one would willingly detract from the high consideration due them as ministers to the better instincts and aspirations of their people. State in the strongest terms the value of their presence and influence among the

---

[1] Mather's account of the trouble, as might be expected, is far from satisfying. He attributes to Mr. Bulkeley some hastiness of speech, and "importunate pressing a piece of charity disagreeable to the will of the ruling elder" (Magnalia, iii. c. 10); by which term he is supposed to refer to Mr. Jones, but ruling elders were selected from the laymen.

The pious Johnson, writing of these times, says: "And verily the edge of their appetite was greater to spirituall duties at their first coming in time of wants, than afterward."

colonists, — the problem was still to be solved. The wolf at the door was first to be met, and other considerations were, not unnaturally, forced to yield their claims for the time.

Concord was not alone in this respect; for, under similar circumstances and for like reasons, Hooker and his followers abandoned Cambridge, to become the founders of Hartford. Of the earliest graduates of Harvard College, a very large proportion qualified themselves to become ministers; but it is amusing to find that, for lack of employment on this side of the water, some went to England to seek their fortune. Mr. Bulkeley's son John, a member of the first class that graduated, — the class of 1642, — took part in this retrograde movement.[1]

The population of the town, in 1644, consisted of about fifty families. "Their buildings," says Johnson, "are conveniently placed, chiefly in one straite street under a sunny banke in a low levell. Their herd of great cattell are about three hundred." In 1640, their exemption from public rates having ceased, the tax assessed upon Concord was £50; and since, owing to the scarcity of money, this tax was payable in cattle or produce, Simon Willard, Thomas Brooke, and William Wood, were appointed by the Court a committee "for valuing horses, mares, cowes, oxen, goats, & hoggs" in Concord.[2]

The following petition was presented, September

---

[1] Winthrop, ii. 294; Hutchinson, i. 107, note.
[2] Mass. Records, i. 291, 295.

7, 1643,[1] by some who joined the plantation in its fifth year : —

"Whereas your humble petitioners came into this country about four years agoe, and have since then lived at Concord, where we were forced to buy what now we have, or the most of it, the convenience of the town being before given out: your petitioners having been brought up in husbandry, of children, finding the lands about the town very barren, and the meadows very wet and unuseful, especially those we now have interest in; and knowing it is your desire the lands might be subdued, have taken pains to search out a place on the north west of our town, where we do desire some reasonable quantitie of land may be granted unto us which we hope may in time be joined to the farms already laid out there to make a village. And so desiring God to guide you in this and all other your weighty occasions, we rest your humble petitioners."

THOMAS WHEELER
TIMOTHY WHEELER
EPHRAIM WHEELER
THOMAS WHEELER, JR.
ROGER DRAPER
RICHARD LETTIN.

Indorsed : "We think some quantitie of land may be granted them provided that within two years they make some good improvement of it."

The following petition, presented May 14, 1645, speaks for all the citizens : —

"To the Wor: ll Governor, Deputy Governor, with the rest of the Assistants and Deputies of the Court now as-

---

[1] This petition and the one immediately following are reprinted from Shattuck's History of Concord (pp. 14-17). Mr. Shattuck must have had the originals, but I have been unable to find any trace of them.

sembled, The humble petition of the Inhabitants of Concord sheweth:

"That whereas we have lived most of us at Concord since our coming over into these parts, and are not conscious unto ourselves that we have been grosly negligent to imploy that talent God hath put into our hands to our best understanding; Neither have wee found any special hand of God gone out against us, only the povertie and meannesse of the place we live in not answering the labour bestowed on it, together with the badness and weetnes of the meadowes, hath consumed most of the estates of those who have hitherto borne the burden of charges amongst us, and therewith the bodily abilities of maney. This being soe eminent above what hath befallen other plantations, hath occasioned many at severall times to depart from us, and this last summer, in the end it, a seventh or eighth part of the Towne went to the southward with Mr. Jones, and many more resolved to go after them, so that maney houses in the Towne stand voyde of Inhabitants, and more are likely to be; and we are confident that if conscience had not restrained, fearing the dissolution of the Towne by their removeall, very many had departed to one place or other where Providence should have hopefully promised a livelihood.

"This our condition we thought it our duty to informe you of, fearing least if more go from us we shall neither remayne as a congregation nor a towne, and then such as are most unwilling to depart, whiles there remayne any hopes of ordinance amongst us, will be enforced to leave the place, which if it should come to pass, wee desire this may testify on the behalf of such, it was not a mynd unsatisfyed with what was convenient, which occasioned them to depart, but meerly to attaine a subsistence for themselves and such as depend on them, and to enjoy ordinances. If it be sayd, wee may go to other places and meete with as many difficulties as here, experience herein satisfies us against many reasons. Such as hardly subsisted with us, and were none of the ablest amongst us, either for labour or ordering their occasions, have much thriven in other places they have removed unto.

"Our humble request is you would be pleased to consider how unable we are to beare with our brethren the common charges, the premises considered.

RICHARD GRIFFIN	ROBERT FLETCHER
JOSEPH WHEELER	WALTER EDMONDS
TIMOTHY WHEELER	WILLIAM HUNT
GEORGE WHEELER	WILLIAM WOOD
JOHN SMEDLY	JAMES BLOOD
THOMAS BATEMAN	JOSEPH MIDDLEBROOKE

These in the name of the rest."

Indorsed: "We conceive the petitioners of Concord should (in consideration of the reasons alledged in this petition) be considered in their rates; but how much, wee leave to those that are appoynted to assess the several towns when any levie is to be made."

The town's rate this year was reduced to £15, payable in cattle, corn, beaver, or money at the option of the town;[1] and the following restriction was placed upon removal from the frontier towns:—

"In regard of the great danger y^t Concord, Sudberry, & Dedham wilbe exposed unto, being inland townes & but thinly peopled, it is ordered, that no man now inhabiting & settleed in any of the said townes (whether married or single) shall remove to any other towne without the allowance of a magistrate, or other selectmen of that towne, untill it shall please God to settle peace againe, or some other way of safety to the said townes, Whereupon this Co^{rt}, or the councell of the comon weale, shall set the inhabitants of the said townes at their former liberty."[2]

The town was in such straits that, in October, on the petition of the inhabitants, Lieutenant Willard

---

[1] Mass. Records, iii. 27, 28. [2] Ibid., ii. 122.

was excused by the General Court from further attendance,[1] for the purpose, it may be guessed, that he might go home to put his stout shoulder to the wheel, and by cheering words raise the drooping spirits of his neighbors.

On October 8, 1655, the town lost one of its foremost men by the death of Thomas Flint. Two years later, Major Willard received, as a reward for his distinguished services to the country, a grant of five hundred acres of land, which he selected and laid out in the southerly part of Groton. Rev. Peter Bulkeley died March 9, 1659; and in November following, Major Willard sold his estate in Concord to Captain Thomas Marshall, of Lynn, and removed to Lancaster, whither he had previously been urged to go, and where he filled a high position. Subsequently he removed to Groton, where his son Samuel was settled as minister; and after the destruction of the town by the Indians, he took up his abode at Charlestown, where he died April 24, 1676, at the age of seventy-one years.

Thus, within a short time, the town was deprived of the three leading men of the first generation. We can imagine the sad retrospection with which the survivors of the original company beheld the oft repeated visitations by which their number was being lessened; but new men came to the front, and the foot of progress was never stayed for an instant.

Since the field afforded by the town of Concord

---

[1] Mass. Records, ii. 44.

was not rich enough for the labors of two ministers, fortunately the right man stayed, free to execute what his judgment dictated. Without doubt, Rev. Peter Bulkeley [1] will always hold the most prominent place in our early history. Born at Odell, January 31, 1583, of gentle lineage, he subsequently became a Fellow of St. John's College, Cambridge, and a Bachelor of Divinity. Succeeding his father in the parish church, he preached for about twenty years, until, with others of the non-conforming clergymen, he was silenced by Archbishop Laud, and turned his face toward the new land of promise lying far away to the westward.

Distinguished by education, wealth, family connection, and religious fervor, his position was a commanding one among his fellow townsmen, and of no small eminence in the colony. At times, wearied and disheartened by the struggle for existence going on all around him, his mind would revert to the quiet scenes of his old home in England, where, in obedience to the voice of conscience, he had relinquished much that was attractive to a man of his training and temperament. His letters show that he felt the loneliness of his position. He says, "I

---

[1] As regards the spelling of the name, a curious perplexity is caused by the careless habits of writing that prevailed in the old times. The first Peter uniformly, it is believed, wrote the name as printed in the text, but his son Edward wrote it indifferently "Bulkely" or "Bulkley;" and Edward's son, Major Peter, commonly, but not invariably, used the form sanctioned by his grandfather. However spelled, the name was undoubtedly pronounced as if written *Buckley*.

am here shut up, and do neither see nor hear;"[1] and again, "I lose much in this retired wilderness in which I live."[2] With advancing age and increasing physical weakness came distrust of "the multitude," accompanied by misgivings that the churches were tending towards too great liberty in religious matters, but his faith in the future of his own town was unshaken until "the spirit struck the hour," and the good man was released from earthly trials. Like the great Jewish leader whose example he loved to follow, he was laid to rest without epitaph or memorial stone, "and no man knoweth his sepulchre unto this day."[3]

Very different but quite as interesting characteristics are presented in the person of Simon Willard, who, equally with the first minister, is entitled to

---

[1] To Thomas Shepard, Feb. 12, 1639. See Shattuck, 154.

[2] To John Cotton, Dec. 17, 1640. The original letter is preserved among the Shattuck papers, in the library of the New England Historic Genealogical Society, in Boston. A comparison with the copy printed in Shattuck's History (p. 154), discloses a serious error; for the printed copy makes Mr. Bulkeley say that there is warrant in the Word for making the doors of the church narrower, whereas in fact he said that the remedy under discussion could not be applied without making those doors narrower than was warranted, — which is quite a different matter. For "narrower. This we have warrant for," read "narrower than we have warrant for."

[3] Dr. Ripley, in his "Half-Century Sermon," said: "There is reason to believe that the three first ministers, viz. Peter Bulkeley, Edward Bulkeley, and Joseph Estabrook, were laid in the same tomb." Again, in the same discourse: "If the spot [Mr. Peter Bulkeley's grave] can be ascertained (which is probable), I would that at least a plain block of granite should there be placed, with his name indelibly inscribed."

honor as founder of the town. Knowledge of men, skill in surveying lands, experience gained by trading with the natives, were qualities that fitted him in a peculiar manner to take the lead in locating the land granted by the colonial government, and fortifying the title by peaceful negotiations with the Indian occupants. As deputy and assistant he was well known in the colony, and by the aid of his influence with those in power, the controversy with Watertown about the eastern boundary was brought to a favorable termination.

As captain of the train-band, Willard directed the military spirit of his neighbors when military distinction was second only to that of the church. He surveyed the lands allotted to the settlers, made their deeds, was arbitrator in their controversies, kept their records, and, last office of all, settled their estates after they were dead. A person like this, — useful in any community, at any stage of its history, — was indispensable to the plantation at Musketaquid. We shall hear of Willard again, holding high command in the Indian wars, and affording much-needed assistance to his former townsmen.

It will always be one of Mr. Bulkeley's strongest claims to our veneration, that, recognizing the supreme value of qualities not his own, he gave generous encouragement and active co-operation in aid of the plans devised by the robust mind of his friend and parishioner. Neither could have been spared; for without Willard, the shrewd, practical man of affairs, the settlement might never have been attempted; but after the enterprise was begun, the end might easily have come in discouragement and loss, had it not been for the pious ministrations, and private as well as public benefactions, of Mr. Bulkeley.

Another distinguished citizen, Mr. Thomas Flint, brought with him from Matlock, — a charming place, not unknown to American travellers, — two thousand pounds sterling,[1] a sum which, measured by its purchasing power, would be equivalent to a much greater amount at the present day. This fortune was liberally expended in building up the infant settlement. His entrance into public life as a deputy was emphasized by an order passed March 12, 1638, that

"the ffreemen of Concord, & those that were not free, wch had hand in the vndewe election of Mr Flint, are fined 6. 8^d a peece."[2]

In 1639, he was appointed to act with Simon Willard and Richard Griffin as commissioners, "to have the ending of small matters this year," — a local tribunal invested with jurisdiction of minor offences and civil controversies involving small amounts. When assistant, in 1649, he showed the austerity of the Puritan by joining with Governor Endicott

---

[1] £1,000, according to Shattuck. But Palfrey (Hist. New England, i. 613, note) and Savage (Winthrop, II. 57, note) both prefer the statement of Rev. Peter Bulkeley, who gives the smaller sum. See Mr. Bulkeley's Letter, 3 Mass. Hist. Soc. Colls., i. 47.

[2] Mass. Records, i. 221.

in a protest against the wearing of long hair, as "a thing uncivil and unmanly, whereby men doe deforme themselves, and offend sober and modest men, and doe corrupt good manners."[1]

Among other dignities, Flint enjoyed the distinction of being empowered "to marry in Concord and Sudbury."

The quiet, uneventful lives of the majority of the early settlers, although interesting in every minute detail to the genealogist or family historian, could not be expected to furnish much that would hold the attention of the general reader. But we shall act wisely if we rescue from oblivion, and preserve in some way, every bit of information that can be obtained concerning them. Their names will occur frequently in the following pages, and the more one can learn of the bearers of those names, the more reason he will have to honor the earnest simplicity that characterized their lives.

Theirs was not the pride of birth, but they fairly represented, in their stern Puritan way, the best of the bone and sinew of English yeomanry, — possessors in a high degree of that pluck and endurance that seem destined eventually to bring the greater part of the world under the dominion of the Anglo Saxon.

The Kentish infusion was very strong in the early population of Concord, and, indeed, of Middlesex County. General Gookin, of Cambridge, magistrate, warrior, and philanthropist; Edward Johnson, the

[1] Hutchinson, i. 143.

founder of Woburn; and our own Major Willard, were conspicuous instances in a multitude of humbler men.

It was matter of great moment to America that, instead of the English law of primogeniture, New England adopted the older rule of the common law, by virtue of which all the children succeeded to their father's estate by equitable division. The same principle existed under a modified form in the custom of Kent known as "gavelkind," and was expressly recognized by William the Conqueror. In Massachusetts, the law gave a double portion to the eldest son, but in other respects the sons and daughters inherited equally.

The proud distinction of the Kentishmen was the tenacity with which they held to their rights and customs, and the unhesitating courage, regardless of difficulties or consequences, shown in their defence. They formed the foremost rank at the battle of Hastings, and made terms with the Conqueror at Swanscombe.[1] Twenty thousand men of Kent followed Jack Cade into camp on Blackheath, for the avowed purpose of punishing evil ministers and redressing the grievances of the people.

[1] The men of Kent were never subdued. The shield of the county bears an unbridled white horse, above the proud motto "Invicta." The chorus in Thomas D' Urfey's famous "Song to the Brave Men of Kent" is a vigorous expression of local pride: —

> "Sing, sing in praise of Men of Kent,
> So loyal, brave, and free;
> 'Mongst Britain's race, if one surpass,
> A man of Kent is he."

It is by no accident that the people of Middlesex County have been equally quick to rise in defence of their rights, and to put down the oppressor; for the people of Middlesex derive their origin, in great part, from the freest and most independent of English counties. The patriots of Concord Bridge, Lexington, and Bunker Hill found their prototypes at Hastings and Swanscombe.

CHAPTER III.

> "They added ridge to valley, brook to pond,
> And sighed for all that bounded their domain."
>
> EMERSON.

THE NEW GRANT, OR "CONCORD VILLAGE."
BLOOD'S FARMS.

FOR reasons the force of which it is difficult for us to appreciate, it was not long before the Concord settlers, individually and collectively, were clamoring for more land. We have already remarked that Thomas Wheeler and others, who came to Concord about 1639, found the most convenient of the lands already given out, and, in 1643, petitioned for a grant of land on the northwest, which was conceded on condition that they improved the grant within two years.[1]

Even after the loss of population caused by the withdrawal of Mr. Jones, land that is now the most productive in town was then deemed inadequate for the few families remaining. We have noticed, in the town's petition of 1645, the pathetic account of "the povertie and meannesse of the place," "the badness and weetnes of the meadowes," the loss of population and resources, and the prevalence of empty houses.[2] The petitioners were considered in their rates, but the true remedy for all troubles was

[1] *Ante*, p. 38. [2] *Ante*, p. 39.

thought to be more land, and petitions to that end were presented in 1650 and 1651. The latter, which lacks signature and date, is here given:[1] —

"To the much honoured governour, the Deputy-governour, with the rest of the Magistrates and the deputies of the generall Court assembled at Boston, the humble petition of the Inhabitants of Concord. Sheweth that whereas wee were the first that in this Jurisdiction began an Inland plantation where the land for most part is more barren than upon the sea-coast, and difficulties greater than where nearness of neighbourhood affords a supply of such things with conveniency as such beginnings stand in need of. Notwithstanding wee have not troubled the Court with petitions for further enlargement only the last yeare wee petitioned for a parcell of land if the same might in any measure be likely to make a village, which upon the request of some to have a farme there wee were content to relinquish, with which farme and some others together with the bounds of Watertown, Sudbury, and the last grant unto Cambridge, wee have now but one small out gate left open, and our land much of it being pine land wch affords very little feeding for cattel. Now the Lord haveing bestowed upon most of us children, which wee had rather should wrestle with difficulties neare unto us than to send them into more remote parts. Our humble petition unto the Court is: they would be pleased to grant us a village from the farme granted the last yeare unto Mrs. Hough unto the bounds of Sudbury, and into the Contrey foure or five miles."

Indorsements: "Concord petition. Refer^d to y^o next Session p Curiam   16 8 51."

"The Deputies thinke meete to graunte this petition for the space of fower miles, provided that they plannt uppon the place which they desire befour any others doo appeare

W^M TORREY CLERK."

"16 (8) 51.   Consented to by the magist^s.

EDWARD RAWSON   Secy."

[1] Mass. Archives, v. 112, p. 397. Erroneously classed with the papers of the year 1685.

If the record above given be considered evidence of a grant, it was upon the express condition that the petitioners should occupy the land before any others; and before anything was done under this order of the Court, Chelmsford was laid out, and Nashoba granted to the Indians. A new petition, or a renewal of the old one in October, 1654,[1] was met with an order that they should make a return into court of "what quantitie of land yet remaynes vndisposed of, which they desire."[2] The following return[3] was made: —

"To the Honored Generall Court assembled at Boston. The returne of the number of acres of land granted as an addition to the Towne of Concord according to the order of the General Court in 1654.

"Whereas the Court was pleased to graunt to our Towne a village some fouer years since upon condition they should improve it before others, but neglecting theire opportunity, the plantation of Chelmsford have taken a good parte of the same, also Nattatawants having a plantation granted him which takes up a good some also, we whose names are subscribed have taken a survey of the rest remayning, and wee finde about seven thousand acres left out, of which Major Willard hath two thousand acres, except a little part of one end of his farme which lyes in the place or parcell of vacant land, that was since given to Shawshine, this tract of land being by the last Court granted to

---

[1] Petition of Robert and Elizabeth Blood in Mass. Archives, v. 39, p. 858.

[2] Mass. Records, ii. 364.

[3] What follows is a reprint from Shattuck (History, p. 38), who appears to have seen a copy of the original, attested by Secretary Rawson "as a true copie compared with original on file as it was exhibited to the Generall Court, May, 1655."

our Towne on this condition that at this Court we should acquaint the Court of the quantitye of what wee have.

> Tho. Brooke
> Timothy Wheeler
> Joseph Wheeler
> George Wheeler
> George Heaward
> John Jones."

On the 23d of May, 1655, the following order was passed, which is here printed from the Massachusetts Records, vol. iii. p. 387: —

"Seuerall of the inhabitants of Concord pfering a petition for the graunt of some land, in answer wherevnto, the Court thinkes meete to graunt them fiue thowsand acors in the place mentioned in their pet͠, p͠vided it hinder not any former graunts."

An order which seems to apply to the same subject is given in vol. iv. part i. p. 237, under date of May 29, 1655, as follows: —

"In ans͠r to the petic̃on of the inhabitants of Concord, the Court doth graunt them five thousand acres of land for feeding, according to theire petic̃on, provided it hinder not any former graunts."

The Indian claim to the New Grant was met and satisfied, December 20th, 1660, in the following manner:[1] —

"An agrement mad betwene the Ingenes of Mashoba and the Towne of Concord as foloweth:

"In Consideration, for the last grant of land to Concord, by the genrall Court for an Inlargment to the Towne; the Towne of Concord doth give to the plantres of Mashoba fiveteen pounds

[1] Town Records.

at six a peny which giueth them full sertisfection in Witnes wherof they doe set to there hands, this 20. of the 10. m? 1660 ;

In the psents of, the marke —) of nssquan: the marke V of
Joseph Wheler marchnt thoms, the marke W of Wabatut. the
John Shipard marke ⌣ of gret James natocotos a blind man.
John Jones the marke) of pompant the marke δ of gomps. John Thomas; and John tahatowon"

A preliminary survey by Thomas Noyes was followed by a new order, reserving two thousand acres out of the number actually found and returned, and granting the remaining three thousand.[1]

"Att A Gennerall Court held at Boston 11th of October 1665

"In Answer to the petition of Concord for an enlargement of their bounds: This Court doe Grant them a tract of land conteyned in a plott returned to this Court under the hand of Ensigne Noyes by estimation the whole being about five thousand acres. Whereof the Court reserveth two thousand acres to be layd out to either Indians or English as this Court shall see meete hereafter to dispose and grant and the remaind^r being about three thousand acres this court doe grant to Concord so as the same doe not abridge any former grant made by this Court and It is ordered that Leiftenant Beers & Leiftenant Noyes lay out the same & make their returne to the next Court of Election."[2]

In pursuance of this order, Richard Beers and Thomas Noyes, in 1666, laid out the New Grant, or Concord Village, as it was called, comprising the

---

[1] It is not so clear as one might wish, but from the return of Beers and Noyes (*post*, p. 54) the inference may be drawn that the three thousand acres here spoken of were in addition to the five thousand granted in 1655.

[2] Mass. Archives, v. 39, p. 860.

present territory of Acton, and portions of Carlisle and Littleton; and made their return the following year.[1]

"At a General Court of Election heald at Boston 15th of May 1667 Humbly sheweth this Honor[d] Court that we Richard Beers of Watertowne and Thomas Noyes of Sudbury, being appointed to Lay out & measure to the Inhabitants of Concord a Tract or Tracts of Land, next adjoining to their first Grant in order to which (wee the aboves[d]) did Lay out & measure unto the Inhabitants of Concord their second Grant being five thousand Acres of Land Granted in the year 1655 next Adjoining to their first Grant, Begining at the southwest Angle of their old Bounds extending their s[d] Southerly Line uppon a norwest point four degrees northerly (according to the meridian compass) two miles & two hundred & eighty Rods, there makeing a right Angle on a bare hill, and from thence a line upon a north east point four degrees easterly, two miles one halfe & fifty Rods, There meeting with Nashoba Plantation Line, Running the Line of s[d] plantation to their Angle, one mile one Quarter & sixty Rods, nearest hand upon an Easterly point there makeing a Right angle, Runing a Line being the Line of the Indian plantation Two miles one quarter and sixty Rods, there being Bounded by Chelmesford Line and Billerica Line, as is more plainely described by a plott, in which plott is contained nine thousand & eight hundred acres of Land, one thousand & eight hundred acres being formerly Granted to Major Willard, the other eight thousand being Granted to the Inhabitants of Concord & Layd out the 5th of May, 66.

  Given under our hands.   RICHARD BEERS,
             THOMAS NOYES Surveyer.

The Court Approves of this Returne
       E. R S."

---

[1] The return is printed from a copy attested by Secretary Addington and entered upon the records of the town.

The town voted, January 27, 1668, that the Enlargement

"shall ley for a ffree Comon; to the psent householdres of Concord; and such as shall hereafter, be approved & allowed; except such psell or psells of it as shall be thought met to make farmes for the use & bennifet of the Towne."

A grant was made to Lieutenant Joseph Wheeler of six hundred and ten acres on Chelmsford line, lying in the form of a triangle, the point towards the northwest, and extending southwest to Nashoba, southeast to Nagog Pond. Wheeler sold this in 1678 to Ralph Shepard.[1] Another tract was occupied for a number of years by John Law and Stephen Law, as tenants of the town, under an annual rent of "one Indian corne," which was customarily paid on the day of the annual town meeting.

At the same meeting, in 1668, it was further agreed that

"all men that have not Comon of there owne for there Cattle, acording to the Towne order shall pay 6d. a best, to those that have Comon to lett to them in there querter, and if there be not Comon to let them; they then to put there Cattle elcewhere."

One year later, on January 12, 1669, a lease was made to Captain Thomas Wheeler, for the term of twenty-one years, of two hundred acres of upland and sixty acres of meadow, lying west of Nashoba Brook; in consideration of which, he agreed to pay a yearly rent of £5 after the expiration of the first

[1] Middlesex Deeds, L. 7, f. 201.

seven years, and to build a house forty feet in length, eighteen feet wide, and twelve feet stud " covred with shingles, with a payer of Chimnes;" also a barn forty feet long, twenty-four feet wide, and twelve feet stud. These buildings were to be left at the end of the term for the use of the town, with thirty acres of land in tillage and sufficiently fenced.

He agreed further, and this was the main purpose of the lease, to receive and pasture the dry cattle belonging to the townspeople, not to exceed one hundred and twenty in number, nor to be fewer than eighty. The cattle were to be marked by their owners, and delivered to Captain Wheeler at his house; and the price was fixed at two shillings a head, payable one third in wheat, one third in rye or pease, and one third in Indian corn. The owners were to " keep the said herd twelve sabboth dayes yearely, at the appointment, & acording to the proportion by the said Thomas or his heires allotted."

The number of cattle received under this agreement fell below the lowest limit, and in January, 1673, the terms of the contract were so modified that Captain Wheeler was entitled to receive one shilling per head.

In 1684, when the depositions already referred to were taken, it was thought expedient to obtain from the Indians new and formal deeds of the land comprised within the New Grant. The deeds then taken are given below. The first one [1] relates to a tract of

[1] Middlesex Deeds, L. 69, f. 57.

one thousand acres, forming the southerly portion of the New Grant.

"To all People to whom these presents may come, Greeting Know ye that We, Mary Neepanaum John Speen and Sarah Speen Dorothy Winnetow Peter Muckquamack of Natick and James Speen & Elizabeth Speen his wife of Waymasset Indians For and in Consideration of a valuable sum of money to us in hand paid by Capt. Timothy Wheeler Henry Woodis James Blood and John Flint The Receipt whereof we do hereby acknowledge and therewith to be fully satisfied and contented have sold and by these presents do sell aliene enfeoffe and confirm unto the said Capt. Timothy Wheeler Henry Woodis James Blood & John Flint of Concord in the County of Middlesex in the Massachusetts Colony in New England for the use and behoof of themselves and the rest of the Proprietors of the said Town of Concord a certain Tract or parcel of Land containing by Estimation a Thousand acres be the same more or less and is situate lying and being within the last Grant of Land by the General Court to the said Town of Concord and is bounded Southeast by Sudbury & the Land of Stow alias [Pompasitticutt] and Northwest by the said Stow running by them upon that Line about a Mile and a Quarter, near to a Hill by the Indians called Naaruhpanit and from thence by a strait Line to the North River at the old bounds of the said Town of Concord unto them the said Timothy Wheeler Henry Woodis James Blood & John Flint for themselves and for the use & behoof of the Rest of the Proprietors of the said Town of Concord to them their heirs assigns and successors forever and we the said Mary Neepanaum John Speen and Sarah Speen his wife Dorothy Winnetow Peter Muckquamuck and James Speen and Elizabeth his wife, do hereby covenant and Promise to and with the foresaid Timothy Wheeler Henry Woodis James Blood & John Flint and the rest of the Proprietors of the said Town of Concord that we are the true proprietors of and have good Right & full power to grant bargain & sell the above granted & bargained premises unto the said Timothy Wheeler Henry

Woodis James Blood and John Flint and the Rest of the Proprietors of the said Town of Concord to them their heirs successors and assigns forever and that the said Timothy Wheeler Henry Woodis James Blood John Flint and the Rest of the Proprietors of the said Town of Concord them their heirs assigns and successors forever shall and may at all Times and from time to time forever hereafter peaceably have hold occupy possess and enjoy the above granted Premises in fee simple, be the same more or less without the Let denial or contradiction of us the said Mary Neepanaum John Speen, & Sarah Speen his wife Dorothy Winnetow Peter Muckquamuck and James Speen and Elizabeth his wife, or any of us or any of our heirs or any other person or persons whatsoever lawfully claiming & having any Right Title or Interest therein or to or in any part or parcel thereof —

In acknowledgment of this our act & Deed we have hereto put our hands and seals this fifth Day of May in the year of our Lord one thousand six hundred eighty & four

Signed Sealed & Del[d] in the presence of	John Speen his mark \ and seal
Moses Parker	Sarah Speen her mark O and seal
Noah Brooks	James Speen and seal
Samuel Wheeler, Jun[r]	Elizabeth Speen her mark X and seal
Benjamin Bohow his mark B	Dorothy Winnetow her mark + and seal
Sarah Bohow her mark G	

John Speen & Sarah his wife James Speen and Elizabeth his wife and Dorothy alias Winnetow acknowledged the within written instrument to be their Act & Deed.

May 5. 1684.   before PET[R] BULKLEY assist."

The following deed purports to convey eight thousand acres:[1] —

"To all People to whom These presents may come Greeting

Know ye that We John Thomas and Naanonsquaw his wife Tasunsquaw The Relict of Wawbon dec[d] and eldest

---

[1] Middlesex Deeds, L. 69, f. 58.

Daughter to Tasattawan Sagamore dec.^d Thomas Wawbon her son Solomon Thomas John Nasquaw James Casumpal Senr and Sarah his wife & Sarah the Relict widow of Peter Conoway Indians for and in Consideration of the sum of one and twenty pounds, fifteen of it long since paid to us [*blank in record*] and the Remainder which is six pounds is now paid to us by Capt. Timothy Wheeler Henry Woodis James Blood & John Flint of Concord the Receipt whereof we do hereby acknowledge and therewith to be fully satisfied and contented have sold and by these presents do sell aliene enfeoffe and confirm unto the said Timothy Wheeler Henry Woodis James Blood and John Flint of Concord in the County of Middlesex in the Massachusetts Colony in New England for the use & behoof of themselves and the Rest of the Proprietors of the said Town of Concord a certain Tract or parcel of Land containing by Estimation Eight Thousand acres be the same more or less and is situate lying and being within the last Grants of Land by the General Court to the Town of Concord and is bounded Southeast by the old bounds of the said Town of Concord and is bounded Easterly partly by Billerica partly by a Farm formerly laid out by Major Willard for himself and partly by Chelmsford till it meets with Nashoby Line and then Westerly by the said Nashoby to the Southeast Corner of the said Nashoby and [then northerly] by the said N[ashoby] till it meets with St[ow] and so bounded northwest by the said Stow till it comes Near to a Hill by the Indians called Naaruhpanit and then running upon a strait Line to the North River at the old bounds of the said Town of Concord unto them the said Timothy Wheeler Henry Woodis James Blood and John Flint agents for the Town of Concord and to the rest of the Proprietors of the said Town of Concord to them their Heirs and Successors and assigns forever and we the said John Thomas and Nasquaw James Casumpat and Sarah his wife and Sarah the Relict widow of Peter Connoway do hereby covenant and promise to and with the foresaid Timothy Wheeler Henry Woodis James Blood and John Flint and the rest of the Proprietors of the Town of Concord that we are the true Proprietors of and have good Right & full power to grant bargain and sell the above granted and bargained premises unto the said Timothy Wheeler Henry Woodis James Blood & John Flint and the rest of the Proprietors of the Town of Concord to them their heirs Successors and assigns forever and that the said Timothy Wheeler Henry Woodis James Blood and John Flint & the rest of the Proprietors of the said Town of Concord them their Heirs Successors & assigns shall and may at all times & from time to time forever hereafter peaceably have hold occupy possess and enjoy the above granted premises in fee simple be the same more or less without the Let denial or Contradiction of us the said John Thomas and Naanonsquaw his wife Tasunsquaw widow and eldest Daughter of Tasattawan Late Sagamore dec.^d Thomas Wawbon Solomon Thomas John Nasquaw James Casumpat Senr & Sarah his wife and Sarah the Relict widow of Peter Conoway or any of us or any of our heirs or any other person or persons whatsoever lawfully claiming & having any Right Title or Interest therein or to or in any part or parcel thereof.

In acknowledgment of this our act & Deed we have hereto put our hands and seals this fourteenth Day of August in the year of our Lord one Thousand Six hundred Eighty and four.

Signed Sealed & Del'd,
in the presence of
Ebenezer Ingolds
Joseph Shambery his mark W
Andrew Pittamey his mark A
Joseph Woolley

John Thomas his mark H and seal
Naanunsquaw her mark W and seal
Tasunsquaw her mark W and seal
Thomas Wabon   and seal
Solomon Thomas his mark S and seal
James Casumpat Senr his mark Z and seal
John Nasquaw his mark T and seal
Sarah the widow of Peter
  Conoway her mark > and seal
Sarah the wife of James
  Casumpat her mark ʘ and seal

Midd. ss. Concord August the 29. 1730 before his Majesty's Court of General Sessions of the Peace appeared Mr. Joseph Woolley and made oath that he was present and saw John Thomas Naanonsquaw Tasunsquaw Thomas Wabun Solomon

Thomas James Casumpat John Nasqua Sarah the widow of Peter Conaway and Sarah the wife of James Casumpat execute the within Instrument as their act & Deed and that he together with Ebenezer Ingolds Joseph Shamberry & Andrew Pittamey at the same time set to their hands as Witnesses to the Execution thereof

Att Saml Phipps Cler. Pacis."

The territory extending down the river north of the original grant, and known as Blood's Farms consisted of three original grants by the General Court to Thomas Allen, Increase Nowell and Atherton Hough, respectively; to Allen and Nowell five hundred acres each; to Hough, four hundred acres. The following instrument[1] refers to the Allen and Nowell grants, as well as to the Winthrop and Dudley Farms which were on the opposite side of the river, entirely outside the bounds of Concord, and within the present limits of Bedford and Billerica.

"A Record of a purchase of the Indians right vnto certaine land, by the parties followeing, the 20th of the 4th month 1642.

An agreement made in the behalfe of Mr Winthrope, Mr Dudley M Nowell, & M Allen about theire farmes lyeing vppon Concord River in manner as followeth, betweene Symon Willard in the behalfe of those gentlemen aforesaid, & Nattahatawants Sachim of the same ground.

The said Symon doth purchase of the said Nattahattawants all the ground wch the Court granted to the forenamed gentlemen lyeing vpon both sides of Concord River, that is Mr Winthrope o^r present Governour one thousand two hundred & sixty Acres, Mr Dudley one thousand fyve hundred Acres on the South East side of the River, Mr Nowell fyve hundred Acres. & Mr Allen fyve hundred Acres on the North East side of the River, & in

---

[1] Suffolk Deeds, L. 1, f. 34.

Consideration hereof, the said Symon giveth to the said Nattahattawants sixe fadom of Waompampege & one wastcoate, & one breeches, and the said Nattahattawants doth covenant & bind himselfe, that hee nor any other Indians shall set traps within this ground so as any Cattle might receive hurt thereby, and what Cattle shall receive any hurt by this meanes he shalbe lyable to make it good

    Witnes   the marke of V Natahattawants
John Mills   the marke of O Winnippin an
the mark W of William Gamlin   Indian that traded for him."
the mark of V Sarah Mills

A portion of Blood's Farms came into the ownership of Robert Blood as early as 1642, and the remaining lands were afterwards acquired by him and his brother John. Robert, who married Elizabeth, daughter of Major Willard, came into possession by purchase from the Indians, and in the right of his wife, of other large tracts extending westward to the Chelmsford line and southward to the Concord bounds.[1] Taken together, these farms formed a large part of the town of Carlisle.

The Bloods described themselves in their deeds as "of Middlesex County," or "living neer Concord." The Farms constituted a distinct territory outside of the regularly authorized plantations, but having no separate civil or ecclesiastical government. The occupants paid their rates in Billerica, but when the Indian troubles arose, they found Concord a more convenient shelter, and paid rates in this town. Billerica, however, recovered judgment for the rates assessed

---

[1] See Middlesex Deeds, L. 12, f. 110.

during their residence here, and Concord was obliged to refund the amount collected.¹ The question of jurisdiction caused new embarrassments, and it was at last declared by the General Court, October 11, 1682, to be a grievance that sundry gentlemen, merchants and others, owned great tracts of land, which were daily increasing in value, but notwithstanding, did not pay to public charges; and it was therefore ordered that such persons should pay to the treasurer of the county two shillings for every hundred acres of land, and in that proportion for smaller amounts. Towns were required to make the assessment upon all such lands lying within their bounds, " and also to assess all countrey grants of lands called farmes belonging to peculiar persons, that lye neerest vnto such toune or tounes." ²

Acting under the authority thus conferred, the Concord constables, armed with tax warrants and supported by a sufficient posse, visited the Farms, and were received by Robert Blood and his two sons with contumelious speeches, accompanied by actual violence to their persons. In 1684, Robert Blood, Senior, was fined £10 and ordered to give bond, for abusing John Wheeler, the constable of Concord, by reproachful speeches, and vilifying his Majesty's authority; and the next year his violent treatment of Constable Eleazer Flagg led to a like punishment.³

¹ Mass. Records, v. 188. ² *Ibid.*, v. 375.
³ County Court Records.

It was on all accounts to be desired, that this state of affairs should not continue. The occupants of the Farms were compelled by law to pay rates in some one town at least, whether they received any benefit or not. They wished for roads, but no one felt either duty or desire to afford them any better facilities of communication with the more thickly settled places. Finally, March 17, 1686, Robert Blood, with the assent in writing of his sons Robert and Simon, negotiated a treaty with Peter Bulkeley, Esquire, Henry Woodis, and John Smedly, Senior, acting in behalf of the town of Concord, by the terms of which it was agreed that Robert Blood should thereafter pay in Concord all civil and ecclesiastical dues and assessments incumbent upon him, and a due proportion of whatever expense there might be in building or repairing the meeting-house.

On the other hand, he and his heirs were to be " from time to time, freed and exempted from all Towne offices," and their waste land was not to be reckoned in their minister rates.[1] It was agreed that convenient roads should be laid out for them at the expense of the town, and no town rates were to be assessed to the Bloods except as above specified.

We have been accustomed to say that, by this agreement the Farms were annexed to, or became a part of Concord, and, on the whole, this view is

[1] It was voted, January 27, 1668, " that all wast lands shall pay only 2ˢ—6ᵈ for the 100 acres men hold; by the yeare to publike charges, tell the Towne see Cause to alter it."

probably correct; for, in 1702, Josiah Blood and Samuel Blood, who lived respectively on Allen's Farm and Nowell's Farm, exchanged deeds in which they described themselves as "of Concord."[1] But it is to be observed that the agreement made in 1686 does not in terms provide that the Bloods' "peculiar" shall be merged in, and be considered part of the territory of the township. And in point of fact we know that, down to as late a date as 1744, when the Concord selectmen, once in three years, issued their notices to the authorities of the adjacent towns, requiring them to send committees to join with committees from Concord, in perambulating the town's bounds, the Bloods also were regularly warned to appear at the appointed time, for the purpose of renewing the bounds between Concord and the Farms.

The new grant to Billerica, in 1656, of land west of the Concord River, made it necessary to define more exactly Blood's Farms and Concord Village. Major Willard's farm of one thousand acres, which he gave as dowry to his daughter, Elizabeth Blood, by deed dated Feb. 23, 1658, was laid out on the northwest of Concord, and on both sides of the present boundary between Acton and Carlisle. A triangular controversy between Concord, Billerica, and Robert Blood, about the boundary line dividing this farm from Billerica, arose in 1683, and was not settled until 1701.

[1] Middlesex Deeds, L. 12, f. 725.

The following document,[1] used in the Blood-Billerica controversy is interesting as forming a part of "the old towne booke," which was partially copied in 1664, but was afterwards unfortunately lost.

"The 21ᵈ May 1660.

A Comittee. Chosen by the Towne of Concord to lay out the Major Willards one thousand acres of land, with the Major himselfe Thomas Brooke Robert ffletcher and George Wheeler: the dimensions of it as followeth

1 The first corner begining upon Chelmsford line runing southward 170 Rods

2 The second line Westward 360 Rods

3. The third line northward meeting with Chelmsford line 390 Rods.

4 The fourth line Eastward along Chelmsford line 640 Rods.

This was don by a mutuall consent of the Major Willard and the Comittee Chosen by the Towne: Witness their hands hereunto

James Hosmore	Thomas Brooke
Thomas Browne	Robert ffletcher
and John Howe	George Wheeler
be witnesses hereunto	
setting to our hands	I consent hereto witness my
James Hosmore	hand
Thomas Browne	Simon Willard
John Howe.	

This is a true Coppy taken out of the old towne booke of Concord in one of folios 30 as attested

John fflint towne Clarke

This copie above written. being Compared wᵗʰ the Towne booke of Concord which was produced & read in Court & Compared wᵗʰ said book by

Edward Rawson Secy."

---

[1] Mass. Archives, v. 39, p. 861. For additional details concerning this controversy the reader is referred to Hazen's History of Billerica, pp. 77-81, and the original papers there referred to.

CHAPTER IV.

> "No ripple shows Musketaquid,
> Her very current e'en is hid,
> As deepest souls do calmest rest,
> When thoughts are swelling in the breast,
> And she that in the summer's drought
> Doth make a rippling and a rout,
> Sleeps from Nahshawtuck to the Cliff,
> Unruffled by a single skiff."
>
> THOREAU.

THE SECOND DIVISION OF LANDS. — DIVISION OF THE TOWNSHIP INTO QUARTERS. — ROADS AND BRIDGES. — BULKELEY'S FARM. — FLINT'S FARM. — OTHER LARGE ALLOTMENTS. — UNDIVIDED LAND. — LAND TRANSCRIPTS. — LOCATION OF HOUSE LOTS. — PETER BULKELEY, ESQUIRE. — SECOND MEETING-HOUSE. — TOWN POUND. — MILLS. — BURYING-GROUNDS.

By the first division of lands, which has already been alluded to, a small portion only of the township passed into the hands of individual owners and became private property. House lots were occupied in the immediate vicinity of the meeting-house and the mill. Large tracts of planting ground, such as the Cranefield, lying behind the hills, Brick-kiln Field, South Field, and large areas of meadow land, such as the Great Meadow, Elm-brook Meadow, Pond Meadow, and Town Meadow, were parcelled out in the first division, three or four acres being allotted to each proprietor. The bulk of the territory remained to be divided, and, apparently, the task was not an easy one.

At a meeting of the town held January 2, 1653, the following votes were passed, in relation to this important matter.

"A meting of the Towne of Concord the 2th of the 11 mo. 1652 about second devitiones as foloweth,

Imp^r it is agreed that 20. acres of land shall be for one Cow Comon (of all the land men hold) and two yearling shall goe for one grown beast, and one horse for one beast, and 4. sheep for one beast.

I^t The bounds of the Towne is devided into three parts; as foloweth: only the hogpeen walke is not to be devided;

Imp^r All on the north sid of the great Rivre shall be for them, on that sid of the same; and all on the east sid to Mr Bulkelyes,[1]

I^t the second part of the devition is on the East sid of the aforesid rivre, beyond Cranefild to Shawshine corner, and to Mr fllints pond to the gutter that comes out thereof, and to the goose pond and along the path that comes to the Towne medow & to the Towne; and the psones to Inioye this part are all the Inhabitants from Mr farweles[2] to the East end of the Towne, also Thomas Brookes is to come in amongst them for two, third pts of his land, and Robert Meriam: Sargent Wheler and Georg Meriam to Joyne with them;

I^t the third pt of [the] devition is from the gutter that comes from Mr fllints pond as aforesaid; to the south rivre & betwen the rivres; and those appoynted for that devition, are the Rest of the towne not beforementioned.

It is agreed that if the mair pt of any of the Companyes shall agree for the laying out of the devitiones as before exprest

[1] Charles H. Hallett's.

[2] Henry Farwell lived a short distance to the eastward of George Heywood's dwelling-house on Lexington Street.

then the minor pt shall be Compeled to agree there to, but in Case the maior pt shall not agree; then any pticuler pson shall not be hendred of ther wright, but they shall have power to call on indeferant man and the Company to whome he belongs shall chose one other, or if they shall refeuse so to doe, then the Townsmen shall choose on man, who with the suerveyer shall indeferantly lay out his or there lands so requiring it, this votted.

It is forther agreed that every pson shall have som, quantity of upland adioyning to his medow, where it is in Comon except som more then ordenary ocation may hender it, and in Case any defarance be therein; it is to be ended by indeferent men; and this is to be pt of there second devition;

It is agreed that second devitiones shall not hender, heighwayes to menes propriaties that they have in pticolers, but they shall be inioyed without charge of purchies to be layed out by indeferent men;

It is agreed that all those that have lat grants of lands given them, shall have three acres for one as others have."

The principal, if not the only, object in view in making this division of the township was to facilitate the equitable distribution of the rest of the land. The process of subdivision went on in the several quarters; but, as usual, property brought with it cares and duties, and very soon it was found necessary for the town to take further action, for the purpose of arranging some details that had not been sufficiently considered, and more especially, to apportion the burden of expense caused by the obligation to make and maintain highways, to build a new bridge over the South River near Nashawtuck, and to keep in repair two other bridges that spanned the river.

Accordingly, "after much agitation there about,"

and "after much wearines about these things," it was voted, March 8, 1654,

> "to chose nine men thre out of ech querter impowred by the Towne to here & end former debat, acording to there best light & discresion & Consience; only eight of the nine must agree to what is determined; or else nothing to be of force; this was voated the 8. of the first mo. 1654. at a publique training, & none voatted to the contrarie, but Georg Wheler, Henry Woodies, Joshuah Edmonds & William buttrike these doe declare there publiqe consent [sic] in this case, Thomas Stow also oposis; The men Chosen by the Towne to this worke are as foloweth;
>
> | | | |
> |---|---|---|
> | SIMON WILLARD, | ENSINE WHELER, | THO. BROOKE |
> | ROBERT MERIAM; | GEO. WHELER, | SARGN BLOOD |
> | JOHN SMEDLY. | THO; BATMAN, | GOG HEAWARD." |

One may see at a glance that this committee was chosen with a due appreciation of the importance of the work in hand; for it was composed of men who were foremost in the town's business, by virtue of their large estates as well as their integrity and good judgment. The vote was passed March 8, 1654, and the committee presented a unanimous report of their doings on the following day.

Twenty acres of meadow were reserved for the minister "in the hogepen walke about annusnake;" and twenty acres of plow-land in the South Quarter, together with a like amount of wood-land in the East Quarter, were to be devoted to the same purpose. Twenty acres of wood-land were reserved "for the publique good of the Towne, lying neer the old hogepeen, at ech sid of the Townes bounds line;" five acres of pine wood-land west of the

North River were appropriated for the use of the North Bridge; and certain persons who were "short in lands" were to have the deficiency made up to them on payment of "12d. p^r acre, as others have don, & 6d. p^r acre if the Towne consent thereto."

They recognize the earlier division of the town into three parts, which they call the North, East, and South Quarters respectively, and define them thus: —

"The limits of ech querter as foloweth,
I^t the north querter by there familyes, are from the north part of the training place to the great Rivre[1] & all on to the north sid thereof.
I^t the Easte querter by there familyes, are from Henry farweles all Eastwards with Thomas Brooke, Ensign Wheler, Robert Meriam, Georg Meriam, John Adomes Richerd Rise.[2]
I^t the south querter by there familyes are all one the south & south weste sid of the mill brooke except those before aesprest, with Luke potter, Georg Heaward, Mihell Wood & Thomas Dane."[3]

Thus it appears that the North Quarter comprised all the land on the north side of the great river and west of the Assabet, and extended to the eastward

---

[1] This term was applied to the Concord River below Egg Rock. *Musquetaquid*, the Indian name of the river, is said to have signified "*grass-grown.*"

[2] John Adams lived on the Almshouse lot; Richard Rice, on the corner opposite the house now occupied by William Buttrick.

[3] Thomas Dane's house stood somewhere between the house lately owned and occupied by Joel W. Walcott and the house of Benjamin Tolman.

The location of the first house-lots of George Hayward and Michael Wood I have been unable to fix; but am inclined to believe that they were on the north and west sides of the Common.

of the great river as far as the northerly end of our Common.

The East Quarter included the territory east of the great river and north of the Mill Brook to the town limits. It also extended southward of the line of the Mill Brook, and seems to have been bounded in this direction by a line running south to Goose Pond, and thence easterly to Flint's Pond and the town bounds. "The East Quarter line" is referred to in descriptions of land, and must at some time have been definitely fixed, but it is difficult now to determine its location.

The South Quarter, also called the Southwest or West Quarter, consisted of the territory bounded on the north by the Mill Brook and the North River, on the east by the East Quarter line, on the south and southwest by the bounds of Watertown and Sudbury, and on the west by the North River.

The following record of the division of wood to the dwellers in the South or West Quarter will afford an example of the methods adopted. The date in the record, "17th . . 52," is obscure, but the division was probably made between January and March, 1653.

"The devisions are to witt from the weast end of the towne meadow; runinge by a hollow to Wallden pond, & to crose the pond to the tope of the Rockye hill,[1] & one the south syde of a swompye meadow, called Dongye hole,[2] & so alonge

---

[1] In Lincoln, a short distance north of the Fitchburg railroad.

[2] This name was applied in several instances to swampy lands shut

the south syde of that valy of wood that runes frome the aforsayd; hole to faier haven, as allso to the south syde, & south end, of a peell of wood: called the Short swompe & so to rune to the River, & for this Devisione there are twellue psons to take to the east syde : & south syde of this devisione & there are seaven to take to the weast syde, which makes neer an equall pportione as apeers, in both pportions after, & this is to be vnderstood, that this first devisione of wood, the limits reach but to the weast end of M^r fllints pond meadow & so to the Riever: homeward within these limitts."

The persons who received land by this division were William Wood, George Wheeler, George Hayward, Luke Potter, Thomas Brooke, John Scotchford,[1] Samuel Stratton, Obadiah Wheeler, John Bellows, Nathaniel Billings, Jr., Thomas Dane, William Wheeler, John Miles, James Hosmer, Simon Willard, Joshua Edmonds, Widow [of Thomas?] Barrett, William Buss, and Thomas Dakin.

But the territorial divisions were not strictly identical with the divisions of the townspeople by their dwelling places and families; for Robert Meriam, George Meriam, Thomas Brooke, Ensign Wheeler, John Adams, and Richard Rice, all of whom lived on Walden street and within the territorial limits of the South Quarter, were included in the company of the East Quarter. And Luke Potter, who lived on the east side of Heywood street, and

---

in by hills. A parcel of land in Nine-Acre Corner is still called "Dunge-hole." The valley mentioned above may now easily be seen from the Fitchburg railroad, the wood having been recently cut off.

[1] Almost invariably written by himself *Scocthford*.

between Lexington street and the Mill Brook; Thomas Dane, whose house lot fronted the Common, together with George Hayward and Michael Wood, were joined with the South Quarter.

The company of each Quarter met at the house of a member, and each one brought in a list of his first division land upon which he claimed second division, and submitted a "proposition" for particular parcels that he desired to own, claiming three new acres for every one that he already possessed. The propositions were, with some exceptions, granted, and the allotments thus made were recorded by the Quarter clerk, some of them being transferred at a later day to the town records.

The report of the nine men disposes of matters relating to highways and bridges as follows: —

"The devitiones of the heighwaies are as foloweth; The north querter are to keepe and maintaine all there highwayes, and bridges over the great Rivre in there querter and in Respecte of there gretness of Chorg there about, and in Regerd of the ease of the East querter, above the Rest in there highwayes, they are to alow the north querter three pound;

I^t the East querter are to keepe & maintaine all there heighwayes, and the bredg ouer the north Rivre [at Derby's] and the heighway there to the heighland by Estimation 3. or 4. rods where the Comisoners of Concord and lanchester [Lancaster] being chosen by there Townes to lay out there heighwayes did appoint it;

I^t the south querter are to keepe & maintaine all there heighwayes & bridges ouer the south Rivre, except that at the north Rivre before exspresed that is laied on the Easte querter the south Rivr bridg [at Hurd's] being to be set, where the aforesaid Comisoners appointed it as there agreement declares;

and all these heighwayes & bridgs are to be maintained forever by the querters on whom they are now Cast. and it is forther concluded that if any damiag shall com to the Towne, by the neglect of any part of the Towne in any part of there wayes that part of the Towne, so niglecting ether bridgs or wayes, shall beare ther damiag and secner the Rest of the Towne."

The highways are more particularly defined as follows: —

"The heighwayes are as folow; the north querter are to make & maintaine all the heighwayes from the training place to the great Rivre with the bridg, and all that is to be done the north sid thereof;

I^t the East querter are to make & maintaine, all the heighwayes from Obadiah Whelers house, allong to the baywards and all the heighwayes at the East end of the Towne, with what heighwayes shall fall in that querter with the north bridg rivr[1] and the way at the end thereof on the further sid, 3. or 4. Rods.

I^t the south querter are to make & maintaine all there heighwayes one the south sid of the mill brooke, with Sudbury wayes as also the bridg over the south Rivr, & the wayes beyond towards the north Rivr, untell it come to the north Rivr, before laid on the East querter."

Officers are provided for, as follows: —

"We doe chose overseeres in ech querter for the faithfull pformance of there duty in that case in all pticolers so far as may condeuce for the profit & good of there said querters, as to make Rats to pay workemen & to see that all psones come in sesonabl time & keep them to there bisines faithfully & keep accounts & so see the worke suffisintly don; and they are impoured to call fitt men & Cattle in there querter to the worke &

---

[1] North River Bridge.

pay them there wages; and if any shall refevse to attend, these nesery workes; there names shall be Returned to the Selectmen of the Towne, who shall Impose findes acording to law vpon all such ofendares in that case; also the overseeres as aforesaid shall keep an exact account of there owne time, expended, and shall have suffisient sattisfaction for the same."

Timothy Wheeler and William Hartwell were made overseers of the East Quarter; for the North Quarter, John Smedly and Thomas Bateman; and in the South Quarter, George Wheeler, James Hosmer, George Hayward, and William Buss.

It was further decided that in making rates the "East end" should be assessed two pence in the pound, "for all menes estate acording as Mr. Bulkelys last Rate was mad;" the North Quarter the same; but the South Quarter, four pence in the pound.

The immunity from public rates, as distinguished from those that were laid for town purposes, had long since ceased, and besides the colony rate and the support of the minister, the expenses of highways and bridges were increasing at an alarming pace, by reason of the general development of the country and the need of better means of communication between settlements, and between widely separated portions of the same township.

In response to a petition for relief from the burden of contributing to the support of so many bridges, a committee appointed by the General Court, and another representing the county of Middlesex, met together and settled this matter of county bridges, April 17, 1660. Their decision increased the amount of a former allowance to Concord by the sum of £10, making the whole £30, and it was ordered that the town should be "free from charges to all bridges extant, save theire own bridges." The committees say further: —

"The three bridgs they foot, and plead upon; are for there owne proper speeal and perticuler consecrnment, for there saw mill; Iron workes & other occationes and not, necessary for the County or Country and may at there pleasur be diserted."

The petition was as follows: —

"To the Right Wor^{ll} the Governor Deputy and Assistants wth the rest of the Members of the honord Generall Co^{rt} mett at Boston Octob^r 18th 1659 the humble Petition & Declaration of the Inhabitants of the Towne of Concord. humbly sheweth, that Whereas there was an order made by the honored Court that each county should mainteyne the bridges wth in it that are County bridges, And we understand that there was something since concluded in the Court concerning the severall Townes in this County of Middlesex bearing the charges of the bridges within their bounds except Mystick Bridge, & that which is betweene Billereeay and Chelmsford, which wee yor petitioners here never consented unto and therefore have divers times made o^r complaint to our County Co^{rt} concerning it, but not being there relieved butt referred by them to the consideration of this honored Court now therefore humbly Intreat that our Condition in this respect may be seriously weighed, and that wee may have such releife as this present Court shall in their wisedom judge just & Equall for us to receive. And that the honord Court may the better discerne what the charge hath beene & is like to be about the County bridges in o^r Towne, bee pleased hereby to understand that the length of the Arch-worke of these bridges over the Rivers which at present is & hereafter must be is about sixty rods, besides all the other charge about them, & severall other smaller bridges which frequently need repaires: For ease in the charge whereof we humbly crave yor helpe. And yor petitioners shall pray for the gracious presence of the Lord with you in all yor weighty occasions.[1]

EDWARD BULKELY.
TIMOTHY WHEELER
ROBERT FFLETCHER
GEORGE WHEELER
WILL^M HARTWELL.

The three bridges maintained by the town at this time were situated, one on the South River at Henry Woodis's mansion, another on the great river at Buttrick's,[2] and the third on the North River, at what is now the Derby place.

The last-named bridge was built to facilitate communication with Lancaster and other western settlements, but was probably not a very elaborate structure, for, in 1663, complaints were made of its condition, which were renewed in 1666. In that year it was carried away by the flood, and the

[1] Mass. Archives, v. 121, p. 32.

[2] Probably it will never be ascertained whether the first bridge was at Nashawtuck or at Buttrick's. The first bridge over the South River is said to have been placed a short distance below the bend in the stream against Mr. Hurd's land, a location afterwards abandoned for the present one, in order to obtain a more direct course for the road to Lancaster. The North Bridge stood until 1793 on the spot now occupied by the Battle Bridge, — if one may suggest a name for the structure that gives access to the statue of the Minute-Man. Undoubtedly, at both of these places, houses were built very early on the further bank, but there is reason to believe that at Buttrick's the river was at first forded at a shallow place just below the mouth of the Mill Brook. The North River was passed by fording at the Hosmer place, before the bridge was built.

county treasurer paid to the constables of Concord £20 "which wer Alowed them by the Court towards ther Bridges."[1]

The Mill Brook was crossed by Potter's Bridge[2] (on Heywood Street), and by Fox's Bridge (near Wayside). On the Sudbury Road, the remains of the Swamp Bridge, of which, with the causeway leading to it, a dam was made in 1691 by Jonathan Prescott and Joshua Wheeler, are still visible on land of Arthur G. Fuller, a short distance to the southeast of Walden Pond. Farther on, towards Sudbury and Watertown, bridges were built at Half-way Brook[3] and at Beaver Dam; and several others of minor importance were scattered about the town, spanning the brooks and rivulets that ran in every direction.

The Indian paths were only a foot broad,[4] and it would seem that ways of moderate width might have been sufficient for the English settlers, who never travelled except on foot or on horseback; but the fathers always had hopes of greater things in the future, and the same record that fixed the site of the first meeting-house informs us also, that it was "ordered that the highway under the hill therough the Towne is to be left foure Rodes broad."

---

[1] County Court Records.

[2] In the description of Luke Potter's land (1666) this is spoken of as "the bridge caled the fort bridge;" but it was known for a long time afterwards as Potter's Bridge.

[3] So-called because it was estimated to be half way between Concord and Sudbury.

[4] Johnson.

This was the first and most important highway, afterwards extended and called the Bay Road, as being an outlet to Cambridge Farms, Charlestown, and Boston. Its width varied from four rods to ten rods, but early in the next century it was reduced within limits that accorded more nearly with the extent and needs of travel.

Leading from the Bay Road to the northeast, were the Billerica Road, which was laid out before 1660,[1] and the highway to Woburn, which was formally laid out between that town and Concord in 1665 by committees representing the two towns.

A highway from Watertown to Concord was laid out in 1638,[2] and the road to Sudbury leading past Walden Pond was in existence in 1648. The course of the most ancient road leading to Watertown and Sudbury was by the lane which runs from Walden Street through the land of George Everett, thence through the woods to the southward of Walden Pond, where it crossed the ravine, and emerged from the woods at the James Baker place, in Lincoln. The road which leads past the Almshouse, stopped at the ditch at the end of the house-lots, and a way that was discontinued long ago gave access to Samuel Stratton's house-lot from the Bay Road, at a point near the Staples place.

The way still known as the "Old Marlborough Road" is very ancient, and may be easily followed.

---

[1] Hazen, p. 89; County Court Records, April 6, 1658.
[2] Watertown Records. See Bond, p. 997.

The "Old Groton Road," leading over the North Bridge, was not formally laid out until 1699, but the action then taken was in great part a relocation and straightening of the old ways and paths already existing in the North Quarter.

The earliest way from the South Bridge to the Derby place ran in a curved line, between Nashawtuck Hill and the house of Charles H. Hurd, to the old Colburn house-lot, and then turning more to the westward, reached the Hosmers', and crossed the river by a ford-way near the railroad bridge. When, however, a bridge was thrown over the river, where it is now crossed, at this point, the commmonly travelled way to and from the town was by the John Hosmer place.

There were "driftways" to Fairhaven and "the Rocks;" and ways were laid out to "Fifty-Acre Meadow," "the Hog Pens," "Virginia," "Mento," "Scotland," "Shawshine Corner," "Dunsdell," "the corner adjoining Watertown," "Mr. Flint's Farm," "the Nine Acres," soon called "Nine-Acre Corner," and other places within the town limits.

A large number of private ways, many of which still exist, were laid out for the accommodation of owners of land, — such as the way to the Great Meadow, and the ways into the Great Common Fields lying east of Lexington Street, one entering near the house of Emeline E. Barrett, on Monument Street, another at Merriam's Corner.

In the second division of lands, Rev. Peter Bulkeley

received a tract of seven hundred and fifty acres that included the Codman place in Lincoln, and to Thomas Flint were assigned a like number of acres extending from Flint's Pond to Beaver Pond and the town bounds, comprising what is now the centre of Lincoln. Flint's Farm was owned and occupied for almost a century by descendants of Thomas Flint and their tenants. These were the largest single tracts granted to any individual.

The deposition of Samuel and Joseph Fletcher, taken in 1734, states that in 1683 and 1684 "there were three separate Families that lived upon a Farm formerly called Buckley's Farm, afterwards called Prout's farm, but is now reputed to be the estate of Charles Chambers, of Charlestown, Esq: the said Farm lyeth upon and in the southerly part of the Town of Concord, &c." The persons named as residents were Thomas Skinner, Thomas Pratt, and Ephraim Roper.[1]

Peter Bulkeley, of London, described as an apothecary and son of the first Peter, sold this farm to Timothy Prout in 1671, for the sum of £45, and Edward Bulkeley, as attorney of his brother, gave "full possession & delivery of Seising by turfe and twigg."[2]

James Blood, father and son, received as part of their second division five hundred acres in one parcel, extending southward from the town line. Henry Woodis and Thomas Stow jointly owned a

[1] Middlesex Deeds, L. 31, f. 494. [2] *Ibid.*, L. 8, f. 328.

tract of six hundred and sixty-six acres, situated south of Fairhaven and east of the river, which was sold in 1660 to Thomas Goble and Daniel Dane for £72, and was afterwards occupied by them.[1]

Large tracts were held for a long time afterwards by the Quarters, or by joint proprietors, in common and undivided; as for instance, the "Great Fields" adjoining the Great Meadow; and the "Twenty Score," which extended to the southward from Bateman's Pond[2] and contained, as the name would imply, four hundred acres, and many other parcels besides, in various parts of the town.

It subsequently appeared that there were a few scattered parcels of common land that, for one reason or another, were not granted by the town at this time, but were disposed of at a much later day.[3]

[1] See deeds in the town records.

[2] Named for Thomas Bateman, who owned land adjoining the pond.

[3] In the town records, under date of May 22, 1732, may be found the report of John Hunt, Joseph Lee, and Nathaniel Ball, who were chosen a committee to "Lay out to the persons that had Land to take up in the old Town of Concord." They found that some small quantities of land were due to the respective heirs of six of the early planters, and grants were voted accordingly. From a report made May 23, 1734, by the same committee, acting under instructions "to make search into the Common Land and Report thereon," it appears that they found yet remaining six pieces of common land, which were surveyed by Stephen Hosmer, and contained altogether two hundred and twenty-six acres and a few rods. Among the parcels of ungranted land then discovered was "a small Island in the crotch of the River below Mr Woodises Rock where the Rivers meet," estimated at a quarter of an acre; also a strip measuring about three-fourths of an acre, extending up the river from where the Minute-Man stands, and lying between the river and the old causeway.

Nine years afterwards, in 1664, the town decided to buy a new record book, and that "what is in the old booke that is vesefull; shall be trancescribed into the new; with all lands which men now hold as there proper wright in ther hands now being." The "latter grants" to particular persons had been "written in paper bookes (as granted) and not recorded in a register booke." Therefore, it was voted that every one should draw up a "trancescripe" of all the lands that he then owned; which statement, after being read and approved at a meeting of his Quarter, should be signed by the Quarter clerk and recorded by the "clarke of the Towne records," as approved by the Town.

The recorded descriptions of land which were brought in under this regulation extend from 1664 to 1673 inclusive, but are chiefly confined to the years 1666, 1668, and 1673; and a careful comparison of these descriptions with each other and with other ancient records, affords a means of constructing, with a fair degree of accuracy, a map of the town, showing the location of the house-lots at the time included between the dates given above.

Concord was no longer a small, compact settlement; for the dwellings now extended eastward, on the line of the great road, to Cambridge bounds, a few were located on the road to Billerica, and others on the further side of the rivers, at the north and west.

After remaining for a short time with his friends near the centre, James Hosmer had moved westward to his farm between the rivers, — a part of which is now occupied by his descendant, Abel Hosmer, — where for a time he was the advanced guard of civilization in the colony. His son James, who was killed by the Indians, at Sudbury in 1675, lived a little to the southward, on land adjoining his father's farm.

George Hayward had sold his house, barn, and land near the mill-pond to Mr. Bulkeley, and had built a house and corn-mill at the southwest, where his descendant still lives.[1]

John Heywood had bought Thomas Dakin's house and barn, and the latter was living on the Lancaster Road beyond the South River. Near him, on the same road, was Michael Wood, and farther on, at Brook Meadow, were Obadiah Wheeler and Edmund Wigly.

Henry Woodis lived on the Willard estate, which he bought of Captain Thomas Marshall. To the westward of him was Francis Dudley (on the Colburn place), and, on the south, John Dakin.

Richard Rice, dissatisfied with his small house-lot and orchard near the centre, had set up his household gods anew on his second-division land, at "the east end," close to the town line.

Richard Temple was bringing up a numerous

[1] George Hayward, Senior, was accidentally drowned, March, 1671. The jury of inquest found, that he was "overthrowne by the strength of the streame and so drownded in the river by the iron workes as he was returning to goe home after he had bien healping william ffrizell over the river in a Canuoe."

progeny at his mill on Spencer Brook, and westward of him were Francis Barker and his son John.

Nehemiah Hunt, son of William and lord of Punkatassett, lived on the estate bought by his father of Rev. Peter Bulkeley, and now owned and occupied by his descendant William H. Hunt.

Tradition places the house of Rev. Peter Bulkeley on the lot now owned and occupied by Charles H. Hallett, on Lowell Street. Thomas Dane owned a house-lot of six acres extending from the burial-hill to the mill-pond. Luke Potter's house-lot consisted of six and one half acres on both sides of Heywood Street (then known as "Potter's Lane"), including the land last occupied by Charles Bowers, and extending across Lexington Street.

Going eastward from this point by the Bay Road, the house-lots came in the following order, occupying both sides of the road and extending to the Mill Brook, — John Farewell, twelve acres, Thomas Wheeler, Senior, thirteen acres, and Moses Wheat, sixteen acres (the Staples place). East of Wheat, on the north side of the road, was the house-lot of William Baker, comprising seven acres. Then, running to the brook, as before, came the lot of Nathaniel Stow, fifteen acres, bought of William Fletcher in 1656, and a lot owned by Peter Bulkeley, Esquire.

Next to Bulkeley was Thomas Burgess, ten acres; then came Francis Fletcher, eight acres, Edward Wright, ten acres, Eliphalet Fox, eight acres, Nathaniel Ball, thirteen acres, William Hartwell, nine acres, John Hartwell, ten acres, and William Taylor, eight and three quarters acres.

Still farther eastward were Caleb and Joshua Brooke, Christopher Woolley and Richard Rice.

John Meriam's house-lot consisted of an acre and one half, situated in the corner made by the Bay Road on the south and the Billerica Road on the west. Joseph Dane and Thomas Pellet occupied one homestead on the Billerica Road.

South of the mill-pond, house-lots were laid out between the corner on Main Street and the Almshouse, — running to the brook or pond on the north, and extending towards the southwest, about as far as Thoreau Street. On the Hastings corner, opposite the Bank, was George Wheeler with eleven acres; and then came Joshua Wheeler, with fourteen acres, Robert Meriam, twenty-six acres (Trinitarian Church), John Wheeler, ten acres and one half[1] (Nathan B. Stow's), Lieutenant Joseph Wheeler, twenty acres (George Everett's), George Merriam, thirty acres (the Bartlett place), Nathaniel Billings, six acres (Nathan Derby's), and Samuel Stratton, twenty-four acres[2] (Almshouse).

On and near Main Street, James Smedly's eighteen and one half acres lay north of, and adjacent to the burying-ground. Going westward, in the order

---

[1] Bought of Thomas Brooke, 1664. Middlesex Deeds, L. 3. f. 169.
[2] Bought of John and Thomas Adams, 1651. Middlesex Deeds, L. 1. ff. 167, 192.

named were John Heywood, four acres (next to the burying-ground), William Buss, seven acres,[1] Edward Bulkeley, eleven acres, John Miles, three acres; and on the south side of the way, John Scotchford, nine acres.

On Monument Street, going north, we find, on the west side of the way, Humphrey Barrett occupying a house-lot of twelve acres (D. Goodwin Lang's); John Jones, eight acres (Sarah B. Prescott's); John Smedly, ten acres (John S. Keyes's); James Blood, father and son, fourteen acres (Elizabeth B. Ripley's).

Over the river, were Boaz Browne (Eli Dakin's), Samuel Hunt (George Keyes's), Thomas Browne (Edwin S. Barrett's), Thomas Bateman (the Edmund Hosmer place), William Buttrick (Joseph Derby's), John Flint (Lewis Flint's).

Dorothy, widow of John Heald, occupied a house-lot of seven acres where the heirs of Stedman Buttrick now live, and her son John had settled a little farther northward. Baptist Smedly lived

---

[1] Heywood and Buss bound their respective house-lots on the south by the highway, and Buss bounds his lot on the west "by Mr Edward Bulkely and the highway." The Bulkeley lot was bounded "north with land of William Buss, east with the highway, south with the highway &c." It would seem therefore, that the road which once ran to the northward of the burying-ground on Main Street, after taking a westerly direction on the hard land, must have turned southward between the house-lots of Mr. Bulkeley and William Buss at a point near the Prichard place, and proceeded thence by a course similar to that of Sudbury Street, but making a bend farther on, in order to reach the South Bridge.

near Franklin Dakin's, and Simon Davis near Abel D. Clark's.

It may be remarked that some names which occur frequently in later years are absent from this list. Lee, Minot, Prescott, Whittemore, and Chandler, had not yet appeared. Several owners of large estates failed to make any return, — among them, Peter Bulkeley, Esq., Simon Davis, John Hoar, Edward Wright, Captain Timothy Wheeler, Thomas Burgess, and Christopher Woolley.

Captain Wheeler lived in the house built by Rev. Peter Bulkeley, and, with George Wheeler, as joint owner, was in possession of most of the real estate left by Mr. Bulkeley,[1] but not including the farm at the southeast, which soon passed into other hands. The house-lot and mill-lot comprised thirty-one acres, lying on both sides of the Mill Brook. If Captain Wheeler did not own the mill privilege at this time (1666), he acquired it very soon afterwards.

John Hoar owned upwards of three hundred acres lying beyond the North River, in the west part of the town, and including land now owned by the Commonwealth. The bulk of this he conveyed, in 1671 or 1672, to Edward Wright, in exchange for an estate in the East Quarter.[2]

[1] See deed of Grace Bulkeley to Timothy Wheeler and George Wheeler, September 30, 1663. Middlesex Deeds, L. 3, f. 128.

[2] Part of the consideration received by Hoar was "all the right title & interest wch Edward Wright of Concord aforesaid husbandman hath or should have in and to certain houses lands & hereditaments &c in the Lordship of Castle Browmick (?) in the Coun[ty] of War-

Peter Bulkeley, called "Esquire," was the most distinguished of Concord men in the later colonial days. He was the son of Rev. Edward Bulkeley, was born January 3, 1641, graduated at Harvard College in 1660, married Rebecca, daughter of Joseph Wheeler, and entered very early upon a public career.

Graduate of the college, and scion of a well-known and highly respected family, he was received without hesitation into the ranks of the colonial aristocracy. When speaker of the House of Deputies, he was chosen to go to England with Mr. Stoughton, as agent for the colony in the matter of the Maine controversy. The mission was a failure, but he rose quickly to be an assistant, and commissioner for the United Colonies; and in 1685, upon the dissolution of the old charter, and his failure to be re-elected assistant, he became a member of Dudley's Council.

High military offices were his, and in fact his whole life, which was comparatively short, seems to have been filled with honors, and devoted to the public service. But, unfortunately, by his associations with members of the aristocratic governing

wick in the Kingdom of England by virtue of a deed of gift made by Edward Wright of Castle Browmick aforesaid to feoffees in trust for the use of Francis Wright sonn and heyre apparent of the said Edward Wright and of Mary Wiggin, daughter of Jno: Wiggin of Aldridge in the Count[y] of Stafford (before the solemnizing of a marriage between the said Francis and the said Mary) & to their heyres &c the said deed of gift being now in the hands of mee the said John Hoare, and beareth date the 27th day of June in the 10th year of King James [1613] &c." See Middlesex Deeds, L. 4, f. 409.

class he became estranged from the simple country folk among whom his childhood was spent, and was induced to support the assumptions of the court party rather than the just claims of the people. The rushing tide of events cast him aside, as one for whom there was no place in the new order of things, and retiring to his country home, he died, May 24, 1688, under fifty years of age, after a protracted illness, and leaving an insolvent estate.[1] According to the historian Hutchinson,[2] "it was said by those who charged Bulkley with too great compliance with court measures, that his sun set in a cloud. He died of melancholy."

At the time of his death he lived "next ye millpond" (perhaps where Dr. Barrett now lives), but owned a farm called "Brook Meadow," lying beyond the South River, with a house and barn on it, and a part or the whole of the Iron Works. The farm, comprising forty-two acres, was sold to Stephen Hosmer.

An increased population, and the hope that the plantation had now weathered the storms that threatened its earlier existence, combined to urge upon the people the need of a more commodious and better constructed building in which to meet on Sundays for worship, and on week-days for lecture or the transaction of town business. Accordingly, at a town meeting held January 27, 1668, Captain Timothy Wheeler, Joseph Wheeler, and John Smedly, were

---

[1] Hutchinson, i. 314.   [2] History, ii. 123.

chosen a committee " to make barganes with workemen, to erecte & buld & finies a new metting house;" and in 1672, as we have already seen,[1] the selectmen were instructed to examine and report whether the contract had been fulfilled, and if so, to adopt measures to keep out the water of the mill-pond, which was always encroaching upon the upland of the Common and wearing it away.[2]

The new house was built on the Common, not far from the spot occupied by the present building, and exhibited the same style of architecture as the old meeting-house at Hingham, built in 1681, which had a roof of pyramidal shape, with dormer windows, and was crowned with a belfry. The bell-rope hung down to the centre of the floor, and the sexton stood midway between the main entrance and the pulpit when he rang the bell to call the people together.[3] In the earlier times the people were accustomed to assemble at the sound of the drum.[4]

---

[1] *Ante*, p. 19.

[2] In 1747, the town sold to Ephraim Jones the Wright Tavern lot, described as "a part of the broken Ground in said Town between the Training Field and the Wast Water (so called) . . . to be improved in such a way and manner as to prevent the Training field from wasting away." Captain Jones paid the town £30, and also gave an obligation " to fill up a part of the remaining broken Ground as is marked out and agreed upon." Middlesex Deeds, L. 89, f. 173.

[3] Palfrey, ii. 58, note.

[4] All meetings for town purposes were held in the meeting-house until a third one was built, in 1712, after which time, for ten years, " the old meeting-house " was devoted to town meetings and the sessions of the courts, and the town bell was suffered to remain in its turret.

In 1719, however, the town voted to build a new house " for the

The town pound[1] stood in the southeasterly corner of the Common, next to the Thayer lot. Its location is fixed by the description in the town records of Thomas Dane's land, and by tracing the title of the Thayer lot, to which the parcel hereafter mentioned as granted to Eleazer Flagg was subsequently added. It appears from the town records of March 7, 1692, that

"Eliazer Flagge of sd town did Request of the towne a peese of Grownd near to the meting house ye bredth of ye pownd all between the pownd & ye mill Brook ajoining to ye Courts and Town meetings," to be thirty-four feet long, twenty-six feet wide, and not less than fourteen feet nor more than sixteen feet between joints. In the following year it was voted that the old meeting-house might be "Improved by the Committee towards the building of the New Town house either by pulling of it down or selling of the same according to their discression." At the same time they were authorized "to set the [new] house where they shall Judge it most Convenient," and they selected a spot adjoining the Common and near the easterly side of the old school-house lot. In 1722 the first town meeting was held in the new building, which was standing in 1775; and although set afire on the 19th of April in that year, it was preserved until the building of the first Court House, on the lot now occupied by the building of the Middlesex Mutual Fire Insurance Company. The weather-vane, bearing the date "1673," that stood on the second meeting-house, and afterwards on the Court House, has been preserved, and is in the possession of Louis A. Surette. A facsimile may be seen in the Concord Free Public Library.

[1] The vote of Groton in 1666 about the building of a pound will perhaps serve to give us an idea of what this inclosure was like: "The said pound is to be made thirty feet square, six sufficient rails in height, not exceeding ten feet in length, the rails are two of them to be pinned at each end, in every length; they [the builders] are to make the gate, and to find the irons, and to hang the said gate, with a lock & key for the said gate for the use of the town, for the aforesaid £2,, 10s. The place to be set up is near the meeting-house." Butler's History of Groton, p. 41.

land y^t was formerly Thomas Danes. and the Inhabitants did then freely Give the sayd litle plott of Ground unto the sayd Eliazer Flagge to set his tan pits upon it as his own land."

This may account for the irregular line of the Common at this corner.[1]

Inferior only to the meeting-house in the estimation of the planters was "the town mill," placed in the middle of the settlement and built by the reverend pastor,[2] in accordance with the terms of an agreement entered into with the inhabitants, who granted Mr. Bulkeley, besides other lands, a tract of thirty-one acres upon which his house and mill stood, and lying between the mill-pond and the river. They gave him, also, the right to raise the water to a perpendicular height of four feet ten inches from the bottom of the mill-trough, and the privilege of digging on the Commons for clay and sand to be used in making repairs.

It is not supposed that Mr. Bulkeley was directly concerned in the management of the mill, for, in 1639, William Fuller,[3] "wch kept the mill at Concord," was fined £3 "for grosse abuse in overtoal-

---

[1] The parcel granted as above set forth, I judge to be identical with that sold by Flagg to William Clark for 28s., July 5, 1717 (Middlesex Deeds, L. 28, f. 255), and described as "one half quarter of an acre more or less bounded south upon the mill Brook East upon Land of said William Clark on every other side upon the Pound Meeting house Green or Common Land."

[2] A deed of William Buss to Grace Bulkeley, dated May 4, 1668, (Middlesex Deeds L. 3, f. 264) recites "the purchase of the towne milne house in Concord, built by the aforesaid Mr Peter Bulkely."

[3] Mass. Records, i. 267.

ing." In 1665 it was kept by William Buss, who was warned by the constable to answer "his want of scales & weights in his mill."[1] A little later it passed into the ownership of Captain Timothy Wheeler, who willed it to his daughter Rebecca Minott; and her husband, James Minott, worked it for many years.

The waters of the Mill Brook, augmented by a ditch leading from the westerly end of Flint's Pond, were stemmed at the place still known as the "Mill-dam," and formed a pond between Walden street and the Common. The old ditch that first conducted Flint's Pond water through our village was easily identified in 1874, and the town water-pipe is laid in it for some distance.

As early as 1664, George Hayward had built a saw-mill, to which he subsequently added a corn-mill, in the southwest part of the town, at what is still known as Hayward's Mills. Ebenezer Prout built a mill on the outlet of Beaver Pond, by reason of which the place was long afterwards known by the name of "Prout's Folly."

Other saw-mills were soon put up in various parts of the township: one by Edward Wright, where the Pail Factory now is; another by Richard Temple, on Spencer Brook; and others at the east and north, wherever sufficient water-power could be obtained, to assist the lumber-men who were bent on subduing the grandeur of primeval growths and diverting them to the uses of a new race.

[1] County Court Files.

After Mr. Bulkeley's death, a difference arose between his widow, Mrs. Grace Bulkeley, and the citizens, concerning the extent of the mill privilege in the centre of the town, and the subject was deemed of sufficient importance to be investigated, in 1667, by a committee appointed by the General Court, on her petition, when the rights of the parties were ascertained and made known.

The committee reported [1] that, after hearing testimony and examining the town records, they found

"a great neglect on Mr. Bulkley's part, in not making his couenant wth the toune so cleare as might haue been necessary for his ovne security, yet so much is acknouledged by seuerall of the inhabitants, wch doe yet speake to the trueth & substance of the same, that ffrom wch wee haue drawne vp these conclusions to present to this honoured Court in refference to the premises: —

1. That the ounors of the sajd mill shall have liberty from tjme to time, & at all tjmes, to rajse the water fowre ffoote tenn inches perpendiccular ffrom the bottome of the mill troffe, as now it lieth at the head of the milne pond, but the wast or low shott not to be made narrower then now it is, or to be raysed higher then to rajse the water (at the head of the pond) to fower ffoot seuen inches ffrom the bottom of the milne troffe before the water runns ouer the wast.

2. What land lyeth vnder water, by reason of the milne pond, at such a head of water as aforesajd, shall be the propriety & propper right of the ounors of the sajd mill for euer, excepting alwayes that land which the toune of Concord haue formerly granted to any of their inhabitants, all wch land each proprietor shall enjoy according to his toune grant after the mill is wholly disannulled.

[1] Mass. Records, iv., pt. ii. 379.

3. The ounors of the sajd mill for euer shall not be liable to sattisfy any damage donn to any person or persons whatsoeuer, by such a head of water kept & majntejned as before sajd.

4. The ounors of the sajd mill foreuer shall enjoy the benefit of all that water wch may be obteyned by any meanes formerly attempted i. e. to the higth of such a head of water as aforesajd, wch water shall not be diverted by any person or persons whatsoeuer.

5. Lastly. The ounors of the sajd mill foreuer shall enjoy priuiledge on the comons for clay & sand convenient for the repaire of the mill damage from tjme to tjme as formerly they haue enjoyed.

Symon Willard
Jno Founell, &
Jonathan Danforth.

The Court approoves of this return."

A prolonged search has failed to disclose any record of the original dedication of the two old burying-grounds to the purpose they have served so long. Both were used as places of burial, and are so designated in the town records, as early as 1673, but the description of Thomas Dane's house-lot bounded on the north by the "buryall hill" was probably made about ten years earlier. The stone bearing the earliest date is that erected on the hill in memory of Joseph Meriam. The date is 1677. There is no monument or epitaph to mark the resting-place of any who died during the first forty-two years.

If the tradition as to the site of the first meeting-house is accepted, we should naturally expect to find that the early families buried their dead as near as might be to their place of public worship, after the manner to which they had been accustomed in their old home.[1] This would account for the use of the hillside; and after the lapse of thirty or forty years, the need of additional space would be felt, and it may be that the inclosure on Main Street, first mentioned in 1673, came into use about that time.

There have been family traditions that one or the other of these grounds was a gift to the town from some ancestor; but these traditions lack confirmation, and it seems quite as credible, in the absence of other evidence of a gift or purchase, that both inclosures consist of land that was never granted or allotted to any individual, and is still owned in common by the inhabitants of the town by virtue of the original grant, subject however, to whatever burial rights persons or families may possess.

The road which was originally laid out so as to pass to the east and north of the burying-ground on Main Street was discontinued March 6, 1693, and the land granted by the following vote of the town to Jonathan Prescott, a large landowner, who lived where Dr. Barrett now lives.

"Then was Granted unto Lt Jonathan Prescote at his Request Jointly by the sayd Inhabitants the highway upon the west side of his house lying between the Berring Plac[e] and the land that the s^d Prescot bought & was formerly Georg Wheelers deceased, from the common Road to the land of James Smedly, wch highway is two Rods wide the sayd Prescote is to maintaine or case to be made up a sufficient fence betwixt the sayd highway now Granted & the burying place, and to maintaine the

---

[1] The first meeting-house in Sudbury stood in what is now the oldest cemetery in Wayland. Drake's Middlesex, ii. 463.

same for ever, and the sayd Inhabitants do Grant the premeses unto s^d Prescote for ever unto him and his heirs upon the sayd condition the day above mentioned." [1]

[1] The following items are added from the town records: —

May 9, 1710, " Whereas there hath beene sum demur in ye Town that ye bounds of ye Buring place on ye hill side by Danill Pellitts have not bene so well looked after as they should and that the s^d bounds thereof be no longer neglected ppounded y^t there be a committe of 3 men chosen in each part of the Town one viz., Ensign Thomas Browne. Sa^t John Wheeler Mr Nathanill Billings: to Requier Danill pellitt to Renue the Lins and stake out the bounds of s^d buring plase; and s^d committe to make Report of their doings to the next town meeting voted on the affirmative."

September 25, 1719, Joseph Dakin was paid £4. 19s. 6d. " in full for fenceing the burying places."

The town voted November 15, 1726, to " fence the burying places," and " that they should be fenced with good Stone wall not less than four feet and [one] half high."

November 25, 1745, " Voted that the affair Relating to the Securing the Bounds of the Burying Place on the Hill, and keeping it from wearing away be Left to the discression of the Selectmen."

April 8, 1746, " Abishai Brown was paid £20 for his making a stone wall on the Lower side of the burying place on the Hill."

CHAPTER V.

> "Alas for them! their day is o'er;
> Their fires are out from hill and shore;
> No more for them the wild deer bounds;
> The plough is on their hunting-grounds;
> The pale man's axe rings in their woods;
> The pale man's sail skims o'er their floods;
> Their pleasant springs are dry."
>
> SPRAGUE.

> "Who liveth by the ragged pine,
> Foundeth a heroic line."
>
> EMERSON.

RELATIONS WITH THE INDIANS. — KING PHILIP'S WAR. — FIGHT AT BROOKFIELD. — NASHOBA INDIANS. — CONSTABLE JOHN HEYWOOD'S RETURN.

FROM the very beginning, the relations existing between the colonists and the natives, their immediate neighbors, portended mischief. The latter, even where they met with kind treatment and the desire to do them justice, as was the case in Concord, were universally despised as heathen, and feared because suspected of being in league with the powers of darkness. "The Indian," says Mr. Emerson, "seemed to inspire such a feeling as the wild beast inspires in the people near his den."[1] The Concord men, under the wise suggestions of Mr. Bulkeley, of

[1] Historical Discourse.

Willard and Flint, showed a desire to live on peaceable terms with their unpleasant neighbors, and a willingness to impart to them such instruction in the elements of Christianity and common decency as seemed best adapted to their condition.

Willard and Flint assisted them in drawing up a code for the regulation of their conduct, very practical in its details, and affording, it is fair to suppose, evidence of what were the native's most easily besetting sins.[1]

In 1654, Thomas Brooke, Senior, of Concord, and William Cowdrey of Reading, were appointed for the County of Middlesex "to sell wine of any sort & Strong liquors to the Indians, as to their judgments shall seeme most meete and necessary."[2] The licensed persons were forbidden to deliver to any one Indian more than a pint of liquor at a time, but what was lacking, by reason of this restriction, was more than made up from irresponsible traders, whose cupidity knew no law. Prosecutions for selling intoxicating liquor to Indians were not infrequent, and there appears to have been no unwillingness on the part of the buyer to say where he obtained it.

The natives were employed to some extent by the English in haying time, and at harvest, but they preferred the more congenial occupations of hunting and fishing, and making brooms, staves, eel-pots, and baskets, for which they found a market

[1] Shepard.   [2] Mass. Records, iii. 369.

among the whites. They also brought to market, in the season, huckleberries, strawberries, cranberries, grapes, and venison.[1] Thus by the exercise of tact and by doing justly, the people of Concord succeeded in preserving the friendly relations established in the beginning, until the outbreak of hostilities in 1675, under the direction of Philip. "No Indian shall come into an English man's house," so ran the old agreement, "except he first knock; and this they expect from the English."[2]

It cannot, however, be said with truth that a like state of feeling prevailed through the colony. The Indians of New England were treated as inferior races have always been treated, whenever they crossed the path of a conquering people. In this case the weaker party, besides being few in numbers, were idle, filthy, and shiftless; but as human beings, they were entitled to some consideration, to say the least. They had stanch friends, like Eliot and Gookin, but it must be admitted that there never was a disposition, on the part of the colonists in general, to see any good in an Indian.

Take a few instances from our own neighborhood:

Thomas Dublet, a Concord Indian, was convicted of an assault upon one of the English, and sentenced to pay a fine of £20, in default whereof he was "to be sold to such as would buy him."[3] This man was

---

[1] Letter of John Eliot, printed with Shepard's "Cleare Sunshine."
[2] Shepard.
[3] County Court Records, Oct. 2, 1660.

subsequently of great service in procuring the release of Mrs. Rowlandson from captivity.

Henry, Indian, servant of James Blood, convicted, on his own confession, of burglary and theft, was sentenced to restore three-fold; but when he expressed a desire to work out the sentence as an apprentice at sea, the court ordered that he should be " disposed of & sold for such time as may availe to perform the sentence of the court," and to pay a fine of forty shillings.[1]

As illustrating the value put upon an Indian's word, Goody Draper, of Concord, was " convicted of selling strong water to Indians, so far," says the cautious scribe, " as Indian testimony may be accounted legall & valid." No penalty was inflicted, except to admonish her " of her evil therein," and to order her " to pay the witnesses their costs, to Davy & his wife, six shillings, and unto Josiah, seven shillings & six pence."[2]

The law prescribed that all cattle should be marked, and each town had its distinguishing brand. The larger animals were collected into a herd and driven to Fairhaven, to Captain Wheeler's farm in the New Grant, or to some other convenient feeding-place.

While the crops were in the ground, swine were herded on a large tract of land near Annursnack Hill, known for a long time as the " Hog Pens." After the crops were gathered the animals were

[1] County Court Records, Feb. 11, 1690.
[2] *Ibid.*, Oct. 6, 1663.

allowed to run at large, but the owner lost all claim to them unless they bore some "ear-mark." This regulation was adopted by the colonial government because it was observed that, whenever the animals had attained to any considerable size, Indians appeared in the settlements with pork to sell.

Suspicions that the English were buying their own property led to the enactment of a law that all swine owned by Englishmen should be marked on their ears, but that the Indians should not mark their swine; and furthermore, if they offered to sell pork to the English they were required to bring at the same time the swine's ears whole, or the meat was forfeited.[1] This regulation would easily commend itself; for not only was it calculated to discourage theft, but the natural result of its enforcement would be, practically, to give the whites the control of the pork market.

The Indian outbreak commonly known as King Philip's War began in June, 1675, and lasted fourteen months, imperilling the very existence of the colonies of Plymouth and Massachusetts Bay.

This town was spared the horrors that accompanied the inroads of the enemy in other less favored quarters. Hither came the jealous occupants of Blood's Farms seeking a shelter from the threatening foe, and the homeless people of Groton and Lancaster found here refuge and relief. No hostile foot carried tomahawk and fagot within the bounds

[1] Mass. Records, iv. pt. ii. 512, 513.

of the original grant, and the old men, women, and children slept undisturbed by the dreadful cry in the dark.

There was, however, no sense of peaceful security. All the men of military age were enrolled, and were constantly employed in manning the garrisons of the frontier and scouting from town to town in small parties. In the fight at the Narragansett Fort, Concord's share of the casualties was George Hayward, killed, and Abraham Temple and Thomas Browne, wounded. A detachment from Concord was decoyed into an ambush at Sudbury, April 21, 1676, and ten were slain. Shattuck[1] was able to ascertain the names of five only, viz.: James Hosmer, Samuel Potter, John Barnes, Daniel Comy, and Joseph Buttrick. The Middlesex Probate Records supply the additional names of Josiah Wheeler, David Curry, and Jacob Farrar.[2]

Isaac Shepard was surprised and slain on his farm near Nashoba, in February; and, on March 10th, according to Hubbard,[3] two men were going for hay at Concord, and one of them was killed. Whether

---

[1] History, p. 58.

[2] Captain Hugh Mason's company from Watertown went to the succor of Wadsworth's command, and their account of finding the bodies of five Concord men on the east side of the river is as follows:—

"On the next day in the morning, so soon as it was light, we went to look for Concord men who were slain in the river meadow, and there we went in the cold water up to our knees, where we found 5, and brought them in canoes to the bridge-foot and buried them there." Mass. Archives, v. 68, p. 224.

[3] History, p. 217.

the statement of the latter occurrence should be considered as a brief allusion to the attack on the Shepards, which had already been noted, is somewhat uncertain; very likely it was nothing but a flying report that reached the historian at Ipswich, and was recorded without any attempt to learn the name of the victim. On the page next following is the detailed account of the killing of Isaac and *Jacob* Shepard.

There is no suggestion either by Hubbard or Shattuck, as to the name of the man who was killed while going for hay, and the whole thing rests upon the statement of an author not celebrated for accuracy, who was writing at such a distance and under such circumstances that it was very easy to confound one place with another, and to record as happening in Concord events which in reality occurred elsewhere.

The story of the attack on the Shepard family is told by the last named author as follows:[1] —

" About the middle of February [1676], *Abraham* and Isaac Shepherd were killed near Nashobah in Concord village, while threshing grain in their barn. Apprehensive of danger, says tradition, they placed their sister Mary, a girl about fifteen years old, on a hill a little distance off to watch and forewarn them of the approach of an enemy. She was, however, suddenly surprised and captured, and her brothers slain. She was carried captive into the Indian settlements, but with great heroism made her escape. While the Indians were asleep in the night, probably under the influence of spirituous liquors, she seized a horse, which they had a few days before stolen at Lancaster, took a saddle from under the head of her Indian

---

[1] Shattuck, p. 54. See also p. 381.

keeper, mounted, swam across the Nashua River, and rode through the forest to her home."[1]

It appears from the Probate Records that, on June 20, 1676, administration on the estate of "Isaac Shepard late of Concord" was awarded to Mary Shepard his "relict widow," jointly with "Abram Shepard her brother." Clearly, then, Isaac was killed and Abraham administered upon his estate.

The widow of the former was Mary, the daughter of Baptist Smedly; and the inventory discloses a respectable property, among other things, "A farme at Nashobe, one house one barn 12 ac^{rs} of broken up land 10 of meadow with the rest of the farme," — all valued at £150.

As the evidence stands, we cannot be assured that more than one man (Isaac Shepard) was killed by

---

[1] Hubbard's History, and a "Century Sermon" preached by Rev. Edmund Foster, of Littleton, in 1815, a copy of which is preserved in the Congregational Library, in Boston, are cited as authorities. The statements contained in the sermon are based expressly upon the account furnished by Hubbard. Hubbard says (History of the Indian Wars, p. 217): "March 10th, at Concord two men going for hay one of them was killed;" and again (p. 218): "Also two men were killed at a farm about Concord, Isaac and *Jacob* about the middle of February, & a young maid that was set to watch upon a hill, of about fifteen years of age, was carried captive, who strangely escaped away upon a horse, that the Indians had taken from Lancaster a little before."

It has been commonly stated on the authority of these two extracts from Hubbard, that three men were killed in Concord by the Indians. It will be noticed, however, that Hubbard gives the name of one of the victims as "Jacob," instead of Abraham; but an examination of the town records and other sources of information fails to disclose any evidence that a person named Jacob Shepard ever lived or died in Concord.

Indians within the limits of Concord. There may have been one more, but our only authority is Hubbard's brief and vague paragraph, to which the researches of Mr. Shattuck added nothing.

But what claims our attention above all else, is the expedition of Captain Edward Hutchinson, undertaken in the summer of 1675, after hostilities had begun in Plymouth. The "Narrative" written by Captain Thomas Wheeler is the epic of colonial times.

Captain Hutchinson was commissioned by the Council at Boston to proceed to the Nipmuck country, so called, in what is now Worcester county, and confer with the Indians there, for the purpose of preventing, if possible, any extension of Philip's influence in that direction. Captain Thomas Wheeler, of Concord, who was already advanced in years, and had commanded the western troop of horse ever since its organization, was ordered to accompany Hutchinson, with an escort of twenty or twenty-five men of his company.

Accordingly they set out from Cambridge, and arrived at Quabaug, or Brookfield, on Sunday, August 1st. Here they received information that the Indians whom they had expected to meet had withdrawn to a place about ten miles distant, towards the northwest. A detachment of four men was sent forward to assure them of the peaceable character of the expedition, and a meeting was agreed upon for the next morning, at 8 o'clock, on a plain within three miles of the town. There was some apprehension of treachery, but prominent citizens of Brookfield not only expressed confidence in the good intentions of the savages, but declared their own willingness to be present at the conference; and Hutchinson decided that the appointment must be kept.

The Indians, however, did not appear, and this fact, together with other suspicious circumstances, led the sagacious Wheeler to think that to venture further would be unwise. But Hutchinson was unwilling to abandon his mission with nothing accomplished, and, in deference to his wishes, the order was given to advance towards a swamp where the savages were supposed to be lurking. As they proceeded, the narrowness of the path, with the swamp on one side and a rocky hill on the other, forced men and horses to march in single file. Suddenly the war-whoop resounded, and the advancing column was assailed by a volley of arrows and bullets discharged from behind trees and bushes, killing eight men, wounding five, and throwing the line into disorder, which was materially increased by the difficulty of turning about or passing by in the straitened passageway.

Captain Wheeler spurred his horse up the hillside, when, finding himself unhurt and perceiving that some of his men had fallen under the fire of the enemy, who were now rushing forward to finish their work, he turned about and dashed boldly forward to attack them. This movement separated him for a few moments from his men. A well-directed shot killed his horse and brought the old man to the ground, wounded, and it would soon have been all over with the brave captain had not his son Thomas, who was also wounded, come to the rescue. Quickly dismounting, he placed his father in the saddle, and ran by his side until he caught another horse that had lost its rider, and so the two escaped with their lives, but suffering severely from their wounds.

This was merely the beginning. Hutchinson had received a wound that caused his death in a few days, and now the task of extricating the command from its perilous situation devolved upon Captain Wheeler. It was performed in masterly fashion. Keeping to the open country and avoiding the woods, they retraced their way, with the assistance of friendly Indian guides, to the village of Brookfield, took possession of one of the largest and strongest houses, and fortified it as best they could.[1]

They had not long to wait before the enemy appeared in superior numbers and attacked the stronghold with vigor. The captain's disability brought to the front Lieutenant Simon Davis, another Concord man, who fought and prayed with a fervor that reminds one of the soldiers of Cromwell. To him, associated with James Richardson and John Fiske, of Chelmsford, the direction of affairs was entrusted.

---

[1] In his certificate given to Joseph and Sampson, Captain Wheeler speaks of their services in "the inn at Brookfield." It is possible that the inn was the building that was chosen for a fortification. See Wheeler's certificate, printed in Gookin's History.

Two men despatched to Boston for assistance were unable to elude the vigilance of the besiegers, and were obliged to return. The Indians piled hay and other combustibles against the side of the house and set fire to them, thus forcing the English to expose themselves in their efforts to extinguish the flames. Their bows shot arrows tipped with "wild fire," which alighted on the buildings within the enclosure and set them afire. To get their combustible materials close to the walls, a remarkable engine fourteen rods long was constructed by the savages, of poles and barrels, which they trundled forward on its menacing errand.

For three days and nights this horrible warfare continued. The besieged were compelled to witness the mutilation of their dead comrades who had fallen outside, and to endure as best they could the jeers and taunts of the foe. Rain came to the assistance of the little band, by putting out the fires of their assailants, and rendering it difficult to kindle new ones. Davis, who is said to have been "of a lively spirit," exhorted his men to remember that God was fighting on their side, and to take good aim before firing. The prayers and hymns of the soldiers, borne out on wings of fire and smoke, were answered by cries of the unregenerate heathen, who gave utterance to hideous groanings in imitation of the singing of psalms.

Twice did brave Ephraim Curtis attempt to make his way through the enemy's line to go for succor.

Twice was he compelled to return baffled. The third time, by great exertions and crawling for a considerable distance on his hands and knees, he succeeded in reaching Marlborough, where he gave the alarm; and on the evening of the 4th, the garrison was overjoyed at the arrival of their old neighbor and friend, Major Willard, with a force of forty-six soldiers and five Indians, who, hearing at Marlborough of their distress, had altered his course to come to their relief. Towards morning, the Indians departed, having first set fire to all the houses except that which sheltered the whites.

Of the Concord men, Samuel Smedly[1] was killed

---

[1] Samuel Smedly was son of Baptist Smedly. His sister Mary married for her first husband Isaac Shepard, who six months afterwards was killed by the Indians on his farm at Nashoba. Two inventories of Samuel's estate are preserved in the Middlesex Probate Records, which say that he was "slean by The Indians at quapoge." They contain, among other items, the following:

"2 horses lost in the Countrys sarvis 06. 0. 0."

"2 horses was kild with him at the flight at quapoge."

In 1693–95, Samuel, son of the Samuel above named, and his aunt, then Mrs. Jewell, convey the homestead owned by their grandfather, Baptist Smedly, to Adam Winthrop, of Boston.

The death of his son was too heavy a blow for the already severely taxed powers of the aged father, and the tragedy was made complete by the death of Baptist Smedly, only a fortnight after the loss of his son. After devising a portion of his real estate to the wife and children of his son-in-law, Isaac Shepard, he says in his will: "furthrmore I give unto them my Grandchild Jabesh Rutter till he come to the age of twenty-one years." The "prizers" who made an inventory of the estate included the following item: "His Grandchild Jabesh Rutter 008. 00. 00." This was probably meant as their estimate of the value of the boy's services until he should become of age, but at first sight the item is somewhat startling.

at the swamp, and Henry Young was shot while looking out of an attic window. It has already been stated that Captain Wheeler was severely wounded, and his son was detained at Brookfield for several weeks by the injuries he had received.

It is easy to believe that the captain and the remainder of his troop received a hearty welcome on their return home. The town kept the 21st day of October, 1675, as "a day of praise and thanksgiving to God for their remarkable deliverance and safe return." Men from Billerica, Chelmsford, and Sudbury took an honorable part in this affair. The services of Ephraim Curtis, of Sudbury, were especially valuable; but we may say with truth that it was a battle in which Concord men were foremost in the display of courage, and the rarer qualities that constitute good leadership.

Our interest in the story is not marred by any doubts concerning the morality of the purpose and objects of the expedition, as is the case when we read of Lovewell's Fight, and other contests, in the eighteenth century. The Indians appear to have behaved very badly from the beginning. They were guilty of an unprovoked and treacherous assault upon a party whose purpose was one of peace and friendship. The mission was an honorable one and faithfully discharged; and Wheeler and his men are deserving of praise for all time, as brave soldiers who acquitted themselves nobly under the most trying circumstances.

Immediately after the engagement at Brookfield, the militia of Suffolk and Middlesex were ordered to hold themselves in readiness to march at a minute's notice. A military magazine was established in Concord, and an able gunsmith was stationed here in October, to repair arms from time to time as might be required. In October it was ordered [1] that

> "Whereas in Concord & the tounes adjacent there is a necessity of a gunnsmith to be resident there, for the fixing vp of armes, from tjme to tjme, during this warr, it is hereby ordered, that Capt Timothy Wheeler be hereby impowred to impresse an able gunsmith, who is to repaire to Concord, who shall carefully and diligently attend that service."

Everything was placed on a war footing, and the Council even passed an order for building "a line or fence of stockadoes or stones" eight feet high, to extend from the Charles River at Watertown to a point on the Concord River in Billerica, an estimated distance of twelve miles. As many ponds as possible were to be included in the line, to form parts of this barrier, which was designed for the protection of the frontier towns against a marauding enemy. It is unnecessary to say that this foolish scheme was never carried into effect; but the fact that it was seriously entertained and once actually adopted by the Council, is a convincing proof of the excited state of men's minds.

The Christian or "Praying" Indians, as they were called, were suspected, probably without reason as to

[1] Mass. Records, v. 54.

most of them, of sharing in the Brookfield treachery, and of sympathy with Philip in his general plan. This belief and the excitement caused by it induced the colonial authorities to order the removal of the Indians of Ponkapog and Natick to Deer Island in Boston Harbor. For want of a sufficient supply of food and fuel at that place the Indians of Nashoba, about fifty-eight all told, were ordered to Concord in November, 1675, — a disposition of them which caused great commotion among the people, for the memory of Brookfield was still fresh, and the sight of an Indian was scarcely endurable.

General Gookin, Mr. John Eliot, and Major Willard were despatched hither by the General Court, to see that the unwelcome visitors were placed under such care and conduct as might quiet and compose the minds of the English. They found that Mr. John Hoar was the only man in town who was willing to take charge of the miserable remnant.

Unpopular as he was, and bitterly sensible of injustice suffered at the hands of the very magistrates who were now desirous of his aid in seeking to extricate themselves from a serious dilemma, he nevertheless came forward in a truly philanthropic spirit and undertook the care of the Indians. He provided for them in buildings of his own, and began the erection of a new workshop near his dwelling-house, where the Indians might be employed by day and secured at night; and other measures were taken to promote their comfort and safety.

But he was powerless to stem the tide of public sentiment. On the first day of February, 1676, the Eames family were massacred at Framingham; eleven days later came the attack on the Shepards; and hostile demonstrations elsewhere on the near frontier filled the settlements with dismal apprehensions.

These events crowding one upon another gave rise among the Concord people to feelings of strong dislike of the Indians living in the town, — feelings which, although, at this distance of time, we are compelled to believe them unwarranted by the facts, and productive of wrong in their manifestation, cannot be considered inexplicable.

Shortly after the murder of Shepard, some of the inhabitants secretly invited Captain Mosley to come with his company and remove the Indians from the town. He appeared in Concord, one Sunday, in response to this invitation, with a detachment of men, and marched into the meeting-house, where the people were assembled for worship.

At the conclusion of the exercises, the captain addressed the congregation, saying that he understood there were some heathen in the town committed to one Hoar, who, he was informed, were a trouble and disquiet to them; and therefore if the people desired it, he would remove the Indians to Boston. No one made any objection, and there were "two or three that encouraged him."

The meeting broke up, and Mosley, followed by

his men and a large number of the townspeople, started for Hoar's house, "which stood about the midst of the town, and very nigh the town watch-house."[1] Arrived there, the captain counted the Indians and left a corporal's guard, Hoar vigorously protesting against all his proceedings as illegal and unwarranted. The next day the captain came, and, upon Hoar's refusal to recognize his authority, broke in the door and carried off the Indians to partake of the discomforts of Deer Island. These events occurred February 21, 1676.

There was some talk made by the magistrates and deputies about this affair, but the fact that Mosley went unrebuked is sufficient evidence that his action was not looked upon with any general disfavor.[2]

It appears from Gen. Gookin's report, made November 10, 1676, that the Nashoba Indians, about fifty in number, had then returned to their plantation and were living there quietly and unmolested. In 1684, the Nashoba Plantation, four miles square, was

[1] Gookin. In 1638, the town was fined five shillings "for want of a paire of stocks & a watchhouse;" and the following year a like fine was imposed "for not giveing in a transcript of their lands," and ten shillings "for neglecting their watch." In 1641, there was another fine of ten shillings "for neglecting watch & not appearance." Mass. Records, i. 267, 284, 317.

Stocks were usually placed near the meeting-house, and in some places that building was used as a watch-house.

[2] For additional details, see Gookin's History, and Hoar's petition, both printed in the Transactions and Collections of the American Antiquarian Society, vol. ii. The original of Hoar's petition is among the Shattuck papers in the library of the New England Historic Genealogical Society.

said to be "inhabited by a parcell of Indians, but for many yeares hath been deserted all dead except some few y^t are dispersed."[1]

In the return made to Governor Leverett, June 13, 1676, by Constable John Heywood, we have an amusing account of the escape of three Indian women and a child from military custody.[2] The anxious official thus deprecates the wrath of his superiors, and at the same time shows the uneasiness that prevailed: —

Concord this 13th: June 1676.

Honord Gouernor Leuert

"Inasmuch as heare has bin a sad accident befallen us through the ocation of nedglegent persons; which had trust Imposed to them; to keep sentery over three old squas & one papoose, these watchmen fell all asleep, and in the meanetime ye squas made theire escape; from them; which may produce a great deale of damage to us y^t are resident in Concord; because we are affraid they are aquainted with ye Condition of o^r towne, & what quantyty of men we have gon out; & which way they are gone; which may prove very obstructive to o^r army in their design; we had a Capt: appoynted over the magaseine; which I thought to be suffitient to give a Charge to 12 men; to keep senternalls over three old squas; I hope yor hono^r will be pleased to take it into Consideration & send us some more strength to suport us from o^r enemies; for we are in dayly fear; y^t they will make an asault on o^r towne; So hopeing yor hono^r Cannot Impute any Blame to him; who wish to yor hono^r ye best y^t may be; by yor hono^{rs} most Humble Servant

John Haywood;
Consta^{ll}."

[1] Mass. Archives, v. 113, p. 193.   [2] Ibid., v. 30, p. 203.

Two days after the receipt of this petition, General Gookin ordered a draft of twenty men, " to march up to Concord for the security of the [word *garrison* erased] magizen there." [1]

[1] Mass. Archives, v. 69, p. 95.

CHAPTER VI.

"... if they threw
Dice charged with fates beyond their ken,
Yet to their instincts they were true,
And had the genius to be men."
                              LOWELL.

" The rough and bearded forester
Is better than the lord."
                              EMERSON.

THE MILITIA. — EDUCATION. — CHARITIES. — MINING AND MANUFACTURES. — PUBLIC HOUSES. — AMUSEMENTS. — FREEMEN. — THE ANDROS REVOLUTION.

OUR study of the colonial times would justly be deemed incomplete, if we failed to touch more particularly upon the military side of colonial life, — to give a glimpse, at least, of the Puritan as a soldier.

In 1636, Sergeant Willard was appointed " to exercise the military company at Concord,"[1] and the town has never been without a military organization since that day.

Every man of military age, except the magistrates, ministers, and deacons, was required to be furnished with arms and ammunition, to appear at stated times for exercise in military duties, or to go on short

[1] Winthrop, ii. 423. Addenda.

expeditions, for service in the outlying garrisons or scouting from town to town.

Sometimes persons were excused from military duty by reason of age, or other infirmity; but it was necessary to apply to the County Court for the privilege of exemption. For this reason, John Smedly was released "from all ordinary trainings,"[1] and Sergeant William Buttrick was excused "from all ordinary trayneings, watchings & wardings."[2] But William Frizzell was exempted on condition of his "paying 2s. 6d. anno to the use of the military company of the Towne where He lives."[3]

A regiment had but one field officer, who was called sergeant-major, and the whole force was under the command of a major-general.[4] The officers of a company were a captain, lieutenant, ensign, and four sergeants. The commissioned officers carried swords, partisans or leading staves, and pistols; and they were elected by the members of the company and approved by the General Court. The sergeants bore halberds. The common soldiers were armed with matchlock or firelock muskets, each with a pair of bandoleers or pouches for powder and bullets. A forked stick was carried, to be used as a rest to assist the aim.[5]

---

[1] County Court Records, June 20, 1676.
[2] *Ibid.*, June 19, 1683. Buttrick's petition, not, as I judge, in his hand-writing, is among the Shattuck papers.
[3] County Court Records, June 25, 1661.
[4] Hutchinson, i. 396.
[5] Palfrey, ii. 49, 50.

The officers were required to be church members, and the military exercises were preceded and followed by prayer offered by the officer in command. The meetings for military exercise had much of the character of town meetings, for it appears by the record that a very important matter — the choice of a committee, in 1654, to make division of the highways — was voted "at a publique training."

Willard was the first to be commissioned captain of the foot company, or train-band. This was May 6, 1646, and Timothy Wheeler was at the same time made ensign.[1] For fifteen years the latter held the responsible post of captain; but in 1677, Peter Bulkeley, Esquire, then in England as agent of the colony, was appointed captain,[2] and subsequently became major.

The General Court ordered, October 12, 1669,[3]

"that such persons living in the frontier tounes wth in the county of Middlesex as are legally capacitated to lyst themselues troopers shall haue liberty to doe the same, vnder Thomas Wheeler, Senio^r, of Concord, whom this Court appoints to be their leiften^t, &c."

This was the beginning of the second troop of horse in Middlesex, "being the westerne troope of that county." Subsequently, in 1671, Wheeler was made captain, Thomas Hinchman lieutenant, and Henry Woodis quarter-master.[4] Two years afterwards, Woodis was made cornet, and Corporal

---

[1] Mass. Records, ii. 146; iii. 62, 63. [2] Ibid., v. 151.
[3] Ibid., v. pt. ii. 439. [4] Ibid., p. 486.

William Hartwell was appointed quarter-master in his place.[1]

In May, 1667, the General Court ordered, that in every town there should be a "committee of the militia," and that fortifications should be erected under the direction of the committee and the selectmen, for the protection of the soldiers and inhabitants.[2] It was thought to be necessary and proper, under stress of the public emergency, to build forts or garrisons on any man's land, without other leave or license than what might be inferred from the terms of the general order referred to.[3]

Like other towns on the frontier, Concord was furnished with a considerable number of garrison-houses, scattered over its large territory, to serve for shelter whenever an alarm was sounded. A more extensive stronghold at the centre served as a rendezvous for the soldiers, who were ordered to assemble here to guard the supplies or for the purpose of preparing for operations elsewhere. Shattuck reports[4] the tradition that one of these garrison-houses stood where Dr. Barrett lives, another near Lewis Flint's, a third near Merriam's Corner, two within the present limits of Bedford, one near the John Hosmer place, and a seventh near the Pope and Lyman farm in Acton.

The following documents illustrate the methods employed to secure a quota from the town: —

[1] Mass. Records, iv. pt. ii. 567.   [2] *Ibid.*, p. 332.
[3] Hutchinson, ii. 67, note.   [4] History, p. 47.

"To the honor^d Council sitting in Boston 3^d 10th 75.

By virtue of a warrant from Maj^r Simon Willard directed to the Comittee of the Militia in Concord requiring them to impresse eleven able souldiers well fited &c: for the service of the Country in the present expedition: The said Comittee have impressed (& accord: to order of the hon^rd Council doe returne the names of) these persons; viz: Joseph Busse, Abraham Temple, Samuel How, John Wood, Joseph Wheeler, Thomas Browne, John Wheeler, Timothy Rice, George Hayward, Stephen Farre & John Taylour, who are at present (most of them & the rest seasonably will bee) fitted well with armes: But severall of them doe want & desire to be supplyed with some cloathing (coates especially) & where they may bee accommodated with them they would understand. 3^d 10th 75.

Yo^r worships humble servant

TIM: WHEELER Capt.
of Concord.

Postscript.

Wee having severall Troopers also impressed in this Towne, & there being a Company of Indians ordered amongst us, wch wee are to take care of: Tis humbly desired, that favor may bee showne us, in the release of some (if it may bee) of the persons abovementioned.

TIM: WHEELER."

[Mass. Archives, v. 68, p. 85.]

"To the Hono:^ble Govr: and Councell now sitting in Boston June 28: 1677

The Request of the Millitia of the towne of Concord

Humbly sheweth that the millitia of the said towne receiveing a warrant from the worp^ll Maj^r Gookin to impress foure men for the service of the Country: and being informed that those that were to be prest were intended onely to scout about Chelmesford; and the said Millitia not being able to obtaine those persons that were intended and desired they sent foure youths promiseing to releive them within one week after they went but so soone as they came to Chelmesford they were conducted to black point where they now remaine.

Our humble request to yo[r] Hon[rs] therefore is: that you will please to consider how unfitt these youths are for the Countryes service: namely Samuell Stratton John Wheat, John Ball: Thomas Woolley:: and that they may be dismissed from the said service: and be returned home with the first that doe returne, so shall we ever pray for y[r] Hon[rs] &c.

Timothy Wheeler Capt
in the name of y[e] Millitia."

[Mass. Archives, v. 69, p. 134.]

The high esteem in which military offices and titles were held, as well as the tenacity with which their possessors clung to them, are well illustrated in the case of William Buss. About a year after the close of Philip's War, it became necessary to reorganize the military forces of the town, which consisted of a train-band of upwards of one hundred and fifty men, besides the horse company, to whose ranks Concord contributed a good number of troopers. The old Indian fighter, Thomas Wheeler, was dead, and Thomas Hinchman was made captain of the troop, with John Flint for lieutenant.[1] Timothy Wheeler, the "ancient captain" of the foot company, was infirm with age, the lieutenant had removed from town, and consequently the burden of military affairs fell upon William Buss, who had been ensign for nearly twenty years, and was now about sixty-five years of age.

[1] Mass. Records, v. 142.

The appointment of Mr. Peter Bulkeley, grandson of the Rev. Peter, to the honorable and responsible office of captain, while still absent from the country and suspected of being too friendly to the court party, did not mend matters. The citizens undertook to remove Buss by electing him constable, hoping thereby to force him to relinquish his military position. But *inter arma silent leges.* The old man refused to qualify for the civil office and indignantly appealed to the Council, who annulled the action of the town and subsequently made Buss a lieutenant. Following is his petition and the order thereon:[1] —

"To the Honoble Governor & Councill now sitting in Boston March 21st 1677-8. The Petition of William Buss of Concord. Humbly sheweth that yor Petitior by Vertue of an order from the Genll Court hath served in the sd towne of Concord as an Ensigne to the foot Company for neare the Space of Twenty yeares: And the Leift· of the sd Company being removed out of the towne: and the ancient Capt of the sd Company being weake and infirme: and the Captaine Lately chosen by the Hono:ble Genll Court being in England: a great part of the Charge of the Millitia in the sd towne remaines upon yor Petitionr: and he being now neare Sixty five yeares old: is much disabled (considering what troubles have beene upon the Country possibly may be Renewed) for mannage of that great Concerne: and now the Inhabitants of the said towne as an Addition to his Trouble have Chosen yor Petitior to the office of a Constable in the sd Towne. and (for what he at present apprehends) are Resolv'd to fforce him to serve in the sd place and office.

Yor Petitior therefore humbly Intreats the ffavor of your honors to Consider the premises: and to pass some order whereby

[1] Mass. Archives, v. 60, p. 187.

he may bee freed from the office and service of a Constable in the said towne   So shall he pray for yor Honors &c

WILLIAM BUSS."

Indorsements: "At a Councell held at Boston March 21st 1677-8.

In answer to the within written petition of William Buss the Councell doo hereby order (that if the towne of Concord have chosen the said Buss Constable for the yeare Ensuing) that the Inhabitants of the said towne forthwith meet and choose another person to serve in the said office: and the said William Buss is hereby declaired free from the said office of Constable.

by order of the Councell   JOHN HAYWARD."

Major-General Gookin represented to the General Court, October 14, 1685, that the Concord train-band had but "one Commissioned officer that officiates in this Company — viz Left. Buss who is very aged[1] & not well able to conduct the affaires of ye great company, therefore having informed myselfe as the fittest man to suply the place of an ensigne for that company, I do propound to the court Humphrey Barret, who is a ffreeman & of ye church at Concord, [illegible] a serjeant of that company, that the court will make him Ensigne of Concord foot company." And he was appointed accordingly.

The return of Samuel Jones, "Clerk of ye bona," made July 2, 1689, states that "the souldiers of Concord" met together, and "by a clear voat" nominated James Minott, captain, Simon Davis, lieutenant, and Humphrey Barrett, ensign. The election of these

---

[1] He was about seventy-three years of age.

officers was confirmed and appointments were made accordingly.[1] But in November following it was

"Ordered by the Representatives That the foot Company of Concord being of the number of on hundred & thre score men & upward; be devided into two Company[s] and that the East quart[r] of the town together wth that part of the south quart[r] southward from that street commonly called Scotchford Lane be of on Company & the North quart[r] of the Town & the Remaining pt of the South quart[r] westward of sd Scotchford Lane be another Company.

Nov:[r] 6th : 1689. EBENEZER PROUT Clerk."[2]

As regards education, it was true, of necessity, that throughout the period of which we are treating, there was little reading of books; but every family possessed and read the Bible, and in some houses might have been found Fox's Book of Martyrs, and a few books of sermons, or commentaries, or controversial tracts. Rev. Peter Bulkeley had a very considerable library for those times, a portion of which he bequeathed to Harvard College. From the instructions received by the selectmen in the year 1672, it appears that the nucleus already existed of a town library. It was enjoined upon those officers "that ceare be taken of the bookes of marters & other bookes, that belong to the Towne, that they may be kept from abeuce [ive] vesage, & not to be lent to a any person more then one month at one time."

It is said,[3] that there was a grammar school in Concord before 1680; but, in the earlier years of the

[1] Mass. Archives, v. 107, p. 166.   [2] Ibid., v. 35, p. 70.
[3] Shattuck, p. 220.

settlement, there could have been no regular instruction of the youth, except what was supplied by the minister and by parents; and it is not likely that there was any school-house, or building specially devoted to school purposes, at any time preceding the gift of Captain Timothy Wheeler, in 1687. Even at a much later date, schools in the outlying districts were kept in the house where the master boarded, and when he changed his quarters, the school also moved with him.

Negative evidence to the same point is furnished by the report of John Smedly and Thomas Dakin, in 1680, that "as for schools we have in every quarter of our town men and women that teach to read and write English when parents can spare their children and others to go to them."[1] In the spring of 1665, the town was complained of, for "not having a lattin Schoole M^r;"[2] and for the next four or five years it was necessary, from time to time, to remind the inhabitants of their want of a school-master, and their supposed inattention to the catechizing of youth.

Our forefathers were no less mindful of the advantages of book learning than the rest of the inland population. They saw stretching out before them a life of severe labor, either in tilling the soil or plying a handicraft. Learned professions, — except the clerical, which was already well filled, — offered no allurements. Operations of trade, or

---

[1] Historical and Genealogical Register, v. 5, p. 173.
[2] County Court Files.

marketing the products of the soil, consisted in most cases of simple barter. There was, in general, no taste or desire for what we should call literature, — luckily, for there was nothing accessible with which to satisfy the craving. The great value of the Bible, considered from a literary point of view, was not much dwelt upon, because of the greater importance attached to it as a collection of authoritative precepts, which, rightly expounded, contained all that was necessary for human beings to know.

Considerations of this kind enable us more readily to understand how an ordinary man or woman in those days might have been content with the discourses of Sunday and lecture-day, without taking the trouble to do much reading at home.

As has been already observed, the business of buying and selling, as ordinarily carried on, called for no complicated mathematical knowledge, or for the keeping of elaborate accounts. Therefore, the art of writing, now universally taught and practised, easily fell into disuse, and became an accomplishment for the few, at a time when all paper was imported from England and letters were not expected, or, when written, were carried by a private messenger at considerable expense.

In 1653, the town subscribed £5 a year for seven years, in aid of Harvard College, and about 1672, the sum of £45 was subscribed towards building Harvard Hall.[1]

[1] Mass. Archives, v. 58, p. 93.

In 1687, the cause of education in Concord received encouragement and support from the public bequests of Captain Timothy Wheeler, who died July 10th, of that year. His will contained the following clause, by which he sought to promote education in the town, and to enlarge the training-place, as well : —

"I Give to the Towne of Concord my house that stands near Eliaz. Fleggs house with the Land that itt stands upon and is joyned to itt; wch is about Three acres; be itt more or Lesse bounded by the Highway on the North East by my Land (vizt) the Gutter and Eliazer Fleggs Land on the North West & South This I say I Give to the said Towne to be Improved as followeth (vizt) ; That about halfe an acre of the said Lott be Laid out to the training place the fence to Run from the Corner of the House to the brow of the Hill upon a straight Lyne ; the Dwelling house with the rest of the Land wth all that is upon itt I give to be Improved for the furtherance of Learning and the Support of a Schoole in the said Towne." [1]

By the same instrument he devised to the town the Ministerial wood-lot, of about forty acres, situated between the Turnpike and the Walden road, "to be from time to time Improved for the use and benefitt of the Ministry of the said Towne."

An indenture [2] entered into, in the year 1688, by

[1] Suffolk Probate Records, v. 10. p. 103. The dwelling-house referred to in the above extract was not the Bulkeley house, which, together with the mill, Captain Wheeler expressly devised to his daughter Rebecca, wife of James Minott.

Of the school-house lot, portions were sold from time to time, until two and one-half acres had shrunk to a lot barely large enough to sustain the building, which is now owned by the Misses Ball and is devoted to the use of the Masonic Order.

[2] Mass. Archives, v. 129, p. 130.

the overseers of the poor, of Boston, with Ebenezer Prout, of Concord, affords evidence of what every young woman was expected to know. The subject of the agreement, described as "a poor Child of the age of Nine years," was bound to serve as an apprentice until she became twenty-one years of age or was married. Prout agreed, on his part, that she should "be taught perfectly to read English, Sew, Spin, and Knit as she shall be capable;" that he would supply her with "wholesome sufficient meat, drink, Apparel, washing, & Lodging;" and at the end of the term, dismiss her "with two new Suits of Apparel throughout, one for Lord's days, the other for working days."

It will be noticed that she was to be taught to read, but nothing is said about writing. Of the first planters, nearly all the men, and some of the women, could write, but their sons and grandsons not infrequently signed by making a mark; and during the first three generations it was an unusual accomplishment in a woman to be able to write her name.

As has been already intimated, we should not judge of their deficiencies, in this or in other respects, according to the standards of our day, any more than it would be reasonable for us to gauge their intellectual powers and attainments by the irregular habits of spelling that prevailed. There was no English dictionary[1] to create or authoritatively recognize a

---

[1] Bailey's English Dictionary, published in 1728, was the first attempt to give a full collection of the words of the language. It was for a long time the only dictionary in use among English speaking people, but was superseded by Dr. Johnson's great work, published in 1755.

standard orthography, and even among scholars, uniformity in spelling was not then deemed the virtue that it now is.

In short, under all the circumstances, it is no cause for wonder, that for a time the practical advantages of learning were so slight, to men of ordinary stations in life, that interest in the education of the young languished and seemed almost dead. All New England was for a while overshadowed by ignorance and credulous superstition, which, probably, in Concord assumed their mildest forms. At all events, we may be thankful that, when the clouds rolled away, and the human mind reasserted itself in a demand for knowledge, no blind delusion had left a permanent blot on the town's escutcheon.

Since Concord has sometimes been called the paradise of poor people, the early charities of the town are entitled to some notice at our hands.

William Halsted, dying in the year 1645, bequeathed

"Unto the poore of the towne of Concord fyve pound to be layd out in a Cow, wch I would have So ordered by the Deacons & my executors that it may be a continual help to such as are in need God giveing a blessing thereunto." [1]

That the testator's wishes were faithfully complied with, appears from the following extracts from the records. The first is dated July 13, 1698.

The Selectmen being enformed of ye great p^rsent want of Thomas Pellit they gave order unto Stephen Hosmer to deliver

[1] Suffolk Probate Records, i. 36.

a Town Cow unto sd pellit for his present supply, who accordingly delivered a cow upon ye account afors{d} unto him sd pellit which cow is of a black couler, a white face with black spotts Round each eye, & sd cow is to continue wth sd pellit so long as sd selectmen Judge necessary."

Again, in 1711, the selectmen ordered Daniel Ross

"to drive ye Town Cow (which was with sd Ross) to Hezekiah Fletcher there to be wintered out att the Town{s} charge which accordingly was done."[1]

When the second divisions were settled, in 1654, it was agreed

"that all poore men in the Towne that have not Comones to the numbar of foure shall be alloued so many as amounts to foure, with what they have all Redy; shall have till they be able to purchis for themselues; or untell the Townesmen shall see Case to take it from them; and bestow it on others that want; And we mene those poore men; that at the psent are householdres."

The will of Robert Meriam, who died in 1682, contains the following clause:

"I give to the poor of the Town of Concord four pounds in Corne."

The early settlers of America were quick to believe stories of marvellous productions and discoveries. Belief in the existence of mines of gold, silver, and other minerals, was ever present to them, and acted as a lively incentive to new efforts. In other quarters, expeditions were planned and conducted by old men in search of the fountain of youth, and in the extract from Johnson already quoted,[2] we are informed

---

[1] See agreement with John Cotton, *Ante*, p. 26. [2] *Ante*, p. 4.

that even the pioneer families of Concord were cheered, on their journey from Watertown, " with hopes of a new and strange discovery, expecting every houre to see some rare sight never seen before."

In many respects, as we have already perceived, their hopes were to be disappointed. It remains for us to explore the attempts that were made to discover valuable minerals within the bounds of Concord.

The legislative body, by a vote passed October 14, 1657, granted to the inhabitants of Concord

" liberty to erect one or more iron workes wthin the limits of theire onne toune bounds, or in any comõon place neere therevnto." [1]

Operations were begun under this authority, but it appears that the franchise was not deemed liberal enough, for, in 1660, the Court made the following order: —

" In answer to the petition of the company in partnership in the iron-works at Concord, the Court judgeth it not meete to graunt theire request, i. e., liberty to digg mine in any mans propriety without theire consent; yett being willing to encourage the petitioners in so good a worke, doe graunt them free liberty to digg mine without molestation in any lands now in the Courts possession." [2]

A company was formed, works were erected at Westvale, where the mill of the Damon Manufacturing Company now stands; and in a few years the proprietors owned more than four hundred acres within the old bounds of Concord, and about twelve

[1] Mass. Records, iv. pt. i. 311.   [2] *Ibid.*, iv. pt. i. 429.

hundred acres, bought, for the most part, of Major Willard, and lying principally in the town's New Grant, but partially in Sudbury.[1]

The bog ore discovered in this territory, specimens of which may still be found, was ascertained to be inferior in quality, and not sufficiently remunerative to the adventurers. Joseph Jenckes was prominent in carrying on the works, the unprofitable character of which may be inferred from the fact that, in the year 1668, Joseph Wormwood, brother-in-law of Jenckes, and employed by him at the iron works, received formal notice from the selectmen that he was not considered a desirable inhabitant for the town, and was requested to depart. This proceeding was strictly according to the statute and custom, and was resorted to, in order to prevent the person so warned from becoming a charge to the town. The reasons assigned for giving the notice in Wormwood's case were, that he had no property in town, and that the prospect for the business in which he was engaged was not considered good.[2]

Peter Bulkeley, Esquire, owned an interest in the works, at his decease, but in 1701 James Russell, of Charlestown, who appears to have become the sole owner of the property, is found conveying parcels to Samuel Wright, John Barker, Jr., Samuel Jones, Ephraim Jones, and Jonathan Knight.[3]

---

[1] Middlesex Deeds, L. 9, f. 70.
[2] County Court Files.
[3] Middlesex Deeds, L. 12, f. 599, 634; L. 13, f. 43.

A deposition which was taken April 9, 1697, and is preserved in the manuscript archives of the State,[1] informs us that one Augustus Leihtenegger "did attend the work of a mine or minerall at a place called fair haven within the Limitts of the Towne of Concord," for the term of six months, under a contract entered into with Herman and Hezekiah Usher, merchants, of Boston ; and that he "did in the winter last past build a bridge at his own charge to facilitate his passage too and from Said worke." A house built for the accommodation of the workmen was called "the Mine house," and the scene of the excavations is still known by the name of Mine Hill. It is situated on the farm of George H. Wright, near the bridge at Nine-Acre Corner, where copper ore is now found in the deep excavation made almost two hundred years ago, in the vain hope, which was cherished by so many of the first planters of New England, that the earth would be found to compensate for its lack of fertility by disclosing mineral wealth.

The road to Shawshine Corner ran across a brook called Tar-kiln Brook, a name not uncommon in the old towns, and arising from the practice of tapping the large pine trees to obtain the material from which turpentine and tar were manufactured.

In estimating the resources of the town, in colonial times, it should be noted that there was little need to go elsewhere for manufactured articles.

[1] Volume 88, p. 147.

Cloth for garments was made at home from the wool of sheep that browsed on Concord hills. The operations of tanning and currying hides, and making the leather into boots and shoes, were all carried on within a radius of a few rods. Carpenters built houses and barns, and made chairs, tables, trenchers, spoons, and various other kinds of wooden ware. Blacksmiths fashioned nails, hooks, hinges, latches, and bolts, to be used in the construction of buildings. Smoking kilns supplied lime and bricks, and three or four saw-mills in various parts of the town were busily clearing the land of the forest growth, and thus supplying a large quantity of lumber for an ever increasing variety of uses.

Upon complaint made in the year 1660, for want of a public house, a license was obtained in October, for Sergeant William Buss, to keep a house of common entertainment[1] at a place on, or very near to, the site of the hotel kept in modern times by Joseph Holbrook.

The application was indorsed by the selectmen as follows[2]: —

"To the hono^red Co^rt meeting at Cambridge Octob^r 2^d 1660.

The hono^red Co^rt may bee pleased hereby to understand that wee, the Selectmen of this Towne of Concord whose names are here under written have beene solicitous to Indeavor the settling of an ordinary-keeper in our towne, and have found much difficulty in securing such an one as wee could rest well satisfyed in for such a place. Butt having p^rvailed wth the Bearer hereof Serjeant Busse to keepe it for this yeare past, wee have also

---

[1] County Court Records.   [2] *Ibid.*

p^rcured him to keepe it for a yeare longer; only hee desireth to bee free from any engagement to sell wine & strong waters. Oct: 1 : 1660.

ROBERT MERIAM
ROBERT FFLETCHER
GEORGE WHEELER
JAMES HOSMER

W^th the Consent of the Rest."

It seems that honest Buss did not lose his repugnance to the business of liquor selling, for in 1664, when the selectmen requested a renewal of his license, they desired that it might be limited to keeping "a house of comon entertainment;" and, as he was not "willing to keepe wine and Liquors," they asked that Robert Meriam might have a license "to retale wine and Liquors for the nessesary use of the towne and travilers." The court granted a general license to Buss to keep a public house, but does not appear to have acted upon the request to license Meriam.[1] It may or may not be encouraging, to learn that the practical treatment of the liquor question at that day involved many of the same difficulties with which later generations have become familiar.

In 1670, the selectmen requested that John Heywood might be allowed "to keep a house of enter tainment for strangers for nights loging, beer, and sider," also that Robert Meriam might be impowered "to sell wine & strongwater to those that are sick or weeke & stand in need of our owne towne,

[1] County Court Files.

& strangers that want." The same year Michael Wood, "clerk of the Iron-works," was licensed to sell strong liquors to the laborers connected with the works.[1]

Two years afterwards, "John Haywood ordnary keeper at Concord renewed his license," and had liberty granted him "to retaile strong waters to travellers & sicke persons," upon giving a bond.[2] He lived on the lot that was occupied, until recently, by the Bigelow Tavern, and we first learn of him as keeper of a public house, in the year 1666.

In attempting to enumerate the amusements of the people of Concord, in colonial times, one is not embarrassed by wealth of materials. It was not merely that anything humorous lacked encouragement, it was actively frowned upon. A profound impression is produced upon the student who, after searching in vain for evidence that the colonists sometimes saw the ludicrous side of things, is compelled to recognize the almost entire absence of humor, that characterizes the records, writings, and books of the period.

Cotton Mather, indeed, perpetrates execrable puns, that provoke merriment by their very poverty of wit; but it is generally true that whatever amuses us in the annals of these times, does so, wholly, because of our altered point of view, and the marked difference of our surroundings. We are led to the belief that the actors in the scenes depicted on the records

[1] County Court Files.   [2] Ibid.

looked upon life as a very serious and sad affair; but not the less did they exert themselves to do their duty according to the light afforded them, with a martyr-like fortitude, the effect of which is enhanced by the dreary back-ground.

Theological and doctrinal discussions had great charms for our ancestors, and the Bible afforded endless themes for conversation. The ordinaries slowly grew into favor as places of resort for the less sober members of the community, who there stimulated their faculties with wine or strong water (this was before the day of New-England rum), and indulged in a style and subjects of conversation somewhat less strict than were allowed elsewhere. The writer has found no indication of the prevalence of any kind of games or sports in Concord, but an apprentice in one of the adjoining towns was complained of by his master, in 1666, for "playing att nine pins & cudgells" at the house of a neighbor, during one entire day, and until nine o'clock at night.

There were, no doubt, pleasant gatherings about the spacious fire-places, when neighbors talked together of the crops and the cattle, and the last story about the Indians was told with bated breath. There is ample evidence that the men, both young and old, were not insensible to the gentle influence of the other sex; for marriages were entered into early in life, families were large, and second and third marriages were not uncommon. An unmarried man of a certain age was regarded with suspicion, and in 1670, Thomas Tally, who had lived four years in Concord, was summoned to court " to answer for his long absence from his wife."[1] Being presented in due form for this offence by the Grand Jury, he submitted the following petition: —

"The Humble petition of Thomas Tally Humbly sheweth That the sayd Tally did intend to have gone for England to his wife the last fall but that a neighbour of Concord went for England and into the same parts where she liveth, by whome, the sayd Tally sent to and for his wife and expects a returne by the same person: and if he have no answer, this returne of the ships he doth intend to go for England at the fall if not before and if the honoured Court shall please beare with him till that time yor petitioner will be farther engaged to pray &c.

THOMAS TALLY."

The magistrates were unmoved by his entreaties, and although poor Tally begged to the last that he might be allowed more time in which to collect the money that was due him, and for further opportunity to hear from his wife, the decree went forth that banished him from the jurisdiction.

Viewed from this distance, the betrothals and marriages wear a sombre and business-like look. Both law and public sentiment regarded marriage as a civil contract and nothing more. The ceremony was not performed by ministers, but by lay magistrates, or persons specially appointed and commissioned for that purpose by the General Court, on the petition of the Selectmen.[2]

[1] County Court Files. [2] See Mass. Archives, v. 35, p. 301.

An account of a marriage contract is preserved among the Middlesex Deeds.[1] Peter Wright, who was one of the parties chiefly interested, was a weaver, and died January 15, 1718, aged fifty-three; therefore, at the time of making the following agreement, he was eighteen years of age. He devised property to the town, which was the nucleus of the fund for the Silent Poor.

"Wee whose names are underwritten do testify that wee being at Edward Wright's house at Concord in New England December 31 1683 the s^d Edward Wright Senr & Widdow Lambson of the same Towne did both of them before us give free consent that Peter Wright son of the s^d Edward Wright & Elizabeth Lambson might joyne themselves in marriage when they pleased observing the Orders here established for that end. And at the same time Edward Wright did give unto his son Peter for his portion before us All his land & meadow on the Easterly side the Brooke,[2] bounded with the Brook, North River, Widdow Lambson's land & John Smedlys land only reserving to himself & his other two sons free liberty to make use of the Timber Brush & Gravell upon that land & the use of one halfe the meadow till Edward Wright Junr & Samuel Wright should flow theyr meadow & the s^d Peter to joyne with them according to his meadow and Widdow Lambson at the same time before us did engage to make her daughter Elizabeths portion worth ten pounds upon her marriage-day with Peter Wright afores^d. What is above written was in the presence & approved by Edward Wright Senr & his wife, Widdow Lambson & all Edward Wrights Sen^{rs} Sons, and Robert Blood for to stand good for the fulfilling of what is abovewritten in all respects, Peter Wright paying to his sister Sarah ten pounds when she

---

[1] L. 9, f. 78.
[2] Land now owned by the Commonwealth, in the west part of the town.

comes to age in common pay as it shall then go between man & man here in Concord. Edward Wright also engaged to make his son Peters portion worth thirty pounds upon his marriage day.

JOHN SMEDLY Senr
JAMES SMEDLY "

Sworn to "18 : 4 : 1684."

We know that the grim surroundings did not altogether quench the frolicsome spirits of children, although, unfortunately, the evidence comes to us from the court records. There, clothed in the quaint idioms that prevailed at the time, is an account of a practical joke played upon a worthy family, who lived nearly opposite to the meeting-house, and, for the promotion of other people's fun, were compelled to forego their Sunday dinner. It was in 1678.[1]

"Thomas Pellet & Mary his wife appearing in court do upon their oaths say & attest, that the last Sabbath day was a fortnight, some young persons being at their house at noon time when the Sacrament was administering their pot being boiling over their fire, when they came to take of the same, they found it much abused, & that tobacco smaller & greater pieces they found therein, whereby the provisions therein was made unfit to be eaten, & that some of their children tasting of some little thereof, became sick & vomited. Also they both add that when they came to take notice of their pot, they observed that Mary Power, Hannah Stannup & Peter Rice did laugh & nicker."

Eight persons were fined for this " rudeness " and " mischeife done to ye victualls of Thomas Pellet on ye Lord's day." In the margin of the record is: " Concord men for spoyling Pellet's dinn^r."

[1] County Court Records.

In the early colonial days, no one could vote, or hold office, or even serve as juryman, until he had been admitted a freeman, and none could be so admitted, except members of the churches.[1] This extraordinary rule was departed from (though slowly and reluctantly), because it was found that a strict enforcement of it would exclude a majority of the adult male population from taking part in the doings of the body politic.[2]

A more liberal practice crept in, by which persons who had taken the oath of fidelity to the commonwealth, were allowed the privilege of voting in military and town affairs, and of holding town office. It was by no means strange, therefore, that before many years the applications to be admitted freemen of the commonwealth almost ceased.

It is, however, interesting to observe that the practice was revived in 1689, after the forfeiture of the old charter, and before the government of the Province was established. In the spring of that year, the selectmen of Concord made the following return of the non-freemen who were free-holders, possessing houses and lands of the yearly value of six pounds.[3]

---

[1] Hutchinson, i. 30; Lechford; 3 Mass. Hist. Soc. Colls. viii. 191, 237.

[2] Winthrop, ii. 209, Savage's note. Hutchinson says that this requirement was continued in force, until the dissolution of the government under Andros, "it being repealed in appearance only, after the restoration of King Charles the Second." History, p. 31.

[3] Mass. Archives, v. 35, p. 352.

"In Concord y⁰ 3 of 1ˢᵗ munth 16⁸⁹⁄₈₈

An acount taken of the nonfrremen which are free holders, whos housing and Lands do amount to the uallew of six pounds rante by the year.

Mʳ Jams Minerd	Nathanell Stow
Danell Dane	Nathaell Harwood
Thomas gobile, S[enior]	Eliphelet fox
Roberd Blood, S	John Ball
John wheler, S	Samuel flecher
Nemiah hunt, S	Timithy Ries
Samuell Davis, S	Samuell Stratten
John Shaperd, S	Johnethen habord
Abraham Tempel	Joshua Wheler
Recherd Tempel	James Smadly
Isaac Tempel	Nathanell Buse
Simon Davis	John wood
Roberd Blood	Abraham wood
Simon Blood	Obadiah wheler
Josiah Blood	John Haward
Judath poter	Thomas Wheler
John Jones	Steuen Hosmer
	John Hartwill

THOMAS: WHEELER:
HOMPHARY BARET
NATHANIEL: BILLING: } Select men
STEUEN HOSMOR
ELIPHELET FFOX

21° March. 1689. Voted by the Court to be ffremen

EBENEZER PROUT, Clerk.

Consent?
Jsᵃ Addington Secʳʸ."

Accompanying this document is a certificate written and signed by the minister of the town, which runs as follows:[1]

[1] Mass. Archives, v. 35, p. 352.

"Concord March 12th 89

All whom yᵉ knowledge of what is here exp'ssed doth concerne may please hereby to understand, that yᵉ psons here named are members in the full comunion of the church; Leiftenᵗ Simon Davis, Leiftenᵗ Jonathan Prescot, Joseph ffrench, Thomas Pellet, Samuel Hunt; Eliezer Illag, Samuel Hartwell, Samuel Myriam, John Wheeler, Samuel How, Abraham Taylor, John Hayward, Nathaniel Ball, Samuel Wheate, Timothy Wheeler, John Myriam, Daniel Pellet; Wittnesse my hand:

EDWARD BULKELY."

"22ᵈ March, 1689.

All above written (Except Daniel Pellet) voted to be ffreemen.

his age being questioneᵈ.   Jsᵃ ADDINGTON Secʳʸ.

EBENEZER PROUT Clerk.

From these interesting documents, taken together, we may infer that the thirty-five men, whose names appear in the first list, were not members of the church, although four of the selectmen of that year are included in the number. Indeed, almost all the early families that survived had a representative on this list of the unchurched, and every name stands for an owner of property, — a man whose interests were thoroughly identified with the prosperity of the town. This return shows us, as nothing else could do, how completely the old forms and regulations had been outgrown and quietly allowed to become obsolete.

It is also seen, with no less clearness, that now, when the old charter had been destroyed by its enemies, albeit under due process of law,[1] and Sir

---

[1] The proceedings against the Massachusetts Company were by information in the nature of a *quo warranto*, based upon supposed neglect

Edmund Andros, as Governor, was sailing the ship of state, with no rudder or compass but his own will, which never yet had coincided with the will of the people whom he was governing, a new interest was felt by the colonists in the forms prescribed by the old charter, under which, notwithstanding its defects, they derived title to all their worldly possessions.

There can be no doubt that great injustice has been done to the memory of Andros;[1] but when revolution had been decided upon, inasmuch as he was the immediate representative of a bad government at home, the people were fully justified in treating him as part of the thing to be reformed.

He had exerted himself to procure the overthrow of the charter, which was revered by the people as

---

or abuse of the company's franchises. The suit was begun in 1683, and judgment of forfeiture was ordered on June 18, 1684, on default of the defendant; but further time was allowed for an appearance. Secretary Edward Rawson did not receive official notice of the court's final decision until July 2, 1685. Hutchinson, i. 305, 306.

A commission from the King arrived in the Rose frigate on May 15, 1686, appointing a provisional government for the colony, consisting of a Council of which Joseph Dudley was to be President.

Sir Edmund Andros arrived on December 9, 1686, in the Kingfisher, bearing commissions as governor of the whole of New England. His government was subverted in April, 1689; and on May 14, 1692, Sir William Phips arrived in Boston with the charter creating the Province of the Massachusetts-Bay in New England, which remained in force until the Revolution of 1775.

[1] "A careful examination of the life of Andros will probably convince the student that he was a brave and loyal servant of the crown, a devout but not bigoted churchman, and very far from being the tyrant that New England traditions have portrayed." Sewall's Diary, i. 175, note.

their palladium. For his own emolument, he increased the fees and other expenses incident to the transaction of public business and the settlement of estates. The Governor and Council laid taxes without consulting those who were to pay them, and town meetings were prohibited, except for the purpose of choosing officers once a year, or to comply with the Governor's orders.

It is possible, though not probable, that these violations of the old order might have been submitted to, in preference to a resort to revolutionary violence; but the smouldering embers of popular discontent were fanned into a destructive flame, when Andros, undoubtedly acting under instructions from the home government, declared all the land titles null and void. Did the colonists urge a purchase from the Indians, he answered that he cared no more for an Indian signature than for "the scratch of a bear's paw." The argument from long-continued occupation, under a claim of right, was dismissed with the answer, that no length of possession could make valid a grant from one who had no title.

With the proverbial timidity of capital, some of the owners of large estates, in Boston and elsewhere, bowed to the Governor's dictum, and asked that their titles might be confirmed to them at a nominal quitrent, which was accordingly done, on the payment of substantial fees. But the mass of the people held aloof from this recognition of the theory that king or courtier could show a better title to the lands that had been reclaimed from the wilderness by the exertions of their fathers, and defended by their own arms. They turned a cold shoulder upon men who, like Samuel Sewall, were in other respects worthy of honor, and in full sympathy with the desire for a return to the old order of things under the colony charter, but had not the courage to risk all that they possessed, in a contest with the representatives of the crown.[1] With characteristic simplicity Sewall writes: "The generality of People are very averse from complying with anything that may alter the Tenure of their Lands, and look upon me very sorrowfully that I have given away."[2]

The Revolution that expelled James II. from the throne of England afforded the opportunity desired by the colonists, who rose almost as one man, to defend their homes and the rights of Englishmen. In 1689, on the Nineteenth of April, an oft-recurring date in American history, the Concord people despatched their military company to Boston, under the command of Lieutenant John Heald, to assist in the revolt.[3] The revolution was accomplished without blood-shed, but a valuable precedent was established for America, as well as for England. For

---

[1] It is believed that no one in Concord petitioned for a confirmation of title, with the exception of Rebecca, widow of Peter Bulkeley, Esquire, who, in 1688, joined with Thomas Hinchman in a petition for the confirmation of their title to " the moiety or one half part of the Indian Plantation called Nashobah." Mass. Archives, v. 128, p. 266.

[2] Diary, i. 231, note.

[3] Shattuck, p. 66.

the first, but not for the last time, on this continent,

> "English law and English thought
> 'Gainst the self-will of England fought."

The overthrow of the Andros administration left the colonists without any legal or *de facto* government, and, true to their instincts, the towns met in convention, on May 22d, to consider the state of affairs. The people of Concord defined their position in a striking and truly characteristic manner. They were duly represented in the convention, which decided to reinstate the government chosen under the charter in 1686, and to wait for orders from the new king and queen in England.[1]

This action of the convention was foreshadowed, two days earlier, in the vote of the freeholders of this town, as shown by the following certificate of the Selectmen[2]: —

"May 20th 1689.

Att a meeting of the ffree-Holders of the Towne of Concord, wee do mutually desire that according as wee have declared ourselves by a writeing sent by the Hands of our representatives. that our old authority chosen & sworn in the year 1686 wth the deputyes then chosen & sent to the court may reasume their places and if that cannot be attained, our desires is that that a councell of war may be chosen & settled by our representitives when met together att boston wth the rest of the representitives of the country.

---

[1] Ebenezer Prout of Concord, was made "Clerk to the Representatives," and as such, signed the order for the removal of Andros to the Castle, on June 6, 1689. Mass. Archives, v. 107, p. 84.

[2] Mass. Archives, v. 107, p. 44.

Signed the date above mentioned being then a generall voat of the freeholders of this Town.

THOMAS WHEELER
STEVEN HOSMER
JOSEPH FRENCH

Select men in ye name of ye Rest."

The votes of other towns were sufficiently firm in their tone, showing a due appreciation of the serious condition of public affairs, and affirming the popular view of the questions involved. They were, however, couched in general terms, and the official communication from the Concord Selectmen, as given above, — ill-spelled and ungrammatical as it is, — was the only formal declaration sent to the seat of government, of readiness to go to war in defence of popular rights.

The emergency was an education. The citizens forgot their dislike of free speech; their minds were lifted out of the range of petty scandal and neighborhood gossip, to loftier considerations of the welfare of the race. They were ennobled by the occasion, and when the rights of Englishmen were assailed, stood shoulder to shoulder, as if they recognized the immense significance of their action to future generations of men.

It was not difficult for the people of Concord to take this stand. It was the way of their ancestors, established long years before in the old country; and the sons were but giving expression, in their day and generation, to the ancient Kentish spirit, which had already become the spirit of Massachusetts, and was destined at a later day to animate a great nation.

"The Puritan Spirit, perishing not,
To Concord's yeomen the signal sent,
And spake in the voice of the cannon shot,
That severed the chains of a continent."

INDEX.

AANTONUISH, 14.
Acton, 54; its eastern boundary, 7, 8, 65; part of, joined to Carlisle, 8.
Adams, John, 71; his house, 71, 73; sells estate to Stratton, 87.
    Samuel, 15.
    Thomas, sells estate to Stratton, 87.
Allen, Thomas, grant to, 61, 65.
Amusements, 140, 141.
Andros, Sir Edmund, Governor, 148; his character and proceedings, 148, 149; his government subverted, 148, 150.
Angier's Mills, 15.
Annursnack Hill, 70, 103.
Atawans, 16. (See Tahatowan.)

BAKER, William, his house-lot, 86.
Ball, John, 125, 146.
    Nathaniel, 32, 83, 147; his house-lot, 87.
Barker, Francis, his dwelling-place, 86.
    John, his dwelling-place, 86; Junior, 136.
Barnes, John, killed by Indians, 105.
Barrett, Humphrey, 20; his house-lot, 88; ensign, 127; selectman, 146.
    Widow, 73.
Barron, John, 35.
Bateman, Thomas, 40, 83; on committee to divide highways, &c., 70; overseer, 76; his house-lot, 88.
Bateman's Pond, 83.
Bay Road, The, 80; house-lots on, 86, 87.
Beaver Dam, 79.
    Pond, 10, 32, 82, 95.
Bedford, 8, 9, 61; plan of, 6; its bounds in part, 10.
Beers, Richard, 53; his return of land, 54.

Bellows, John, 73.
Bennett, James, 35.
Berry Corner, 8.
Bigelow Tavern, 140.
Billerica, 6, 54, 61, 84, 113, 114; extracts from its records, 9; bounds renewed with, 9; old line of, 6, 10; bridge, 77; road, 80; old line of, 6, 10; collects rates of the Bloods, 62; new grant to, 65; controversy with Concord and the Bloods, 65, 66.
Billings, John, 20.
    Nathaniel, 99; his house-lot, 87; selectman, 146; Junior, 73.
Births, record of, 21.
Blackbirds, destruction of, 19.
Black Point, 125.
Blood, Elizabeth, 51, 65.
    James, 40, 57, 59; sergeant, on committee to divide highways, &c., 70; his second division, 82; his house-lot, 88; his servant, 103; Junior, his second division, 82; his house-lot, 88.
    John, part-owner of Blood's Farms, 62.
    Josiah, 65, 146.
    Robert, 143, 146; his petition, 51; acquires land, 62; pays rates in Concord and Billerica, 62-64; assaults Concord officers, 63; his agreement with Concord, 64; his controversy with Concord and Billerica about bounds, 65, 66; Junior, 63, 64, 146.
    Samuel, 65.
    Simon, 64, 146.
Blood's Farms, bounds of, 6; how acquired, 61, 62; taxed by Concord, 63; annexation of, 64, 65; their bounds, how renewed, 65; occupants seek shelter in Concord, 104.
Bohow, Benjamin, 58.
    Sarah, 58.
Books, belonging to town, 19, 128; reading of, 130.
Boston, road to, 80.
Brick-kiln field, 19, 67.
Bridge, foot, over North River, 19; over South River, 69, 70; North River, land reserved for, 70; assigned to East Quarter, 74; carried away by flood, 78.
Bridges, support of, 69; assigned to the quarters, 74; county, 77; their location, 77, 78; over Mill Brook, &c., 79; allowance for, 79.
Brooke, Caleb, his dwelling-place, 87.
    Gershom, 20.
    Joshua, 20; his dwelling-place, 87.
    Thomas, 1; on committee for valuing cattle, 37; to divide highways, &c., 70; other committees, 52, 66; takes second division in East Quarter, 68, 71; land assigned to, 73; sells estate to Wheeler, 87; licensed to sell liquor to Indians, 101.

Brookfield, fight at, 108-113.
Brook Meadow, 85; farm so called, 91.
Brooks, Noah, 58.
Browmick, Castle, 89.
Brown, Abishai, fences Hill Burying-Ground, 99.
Browne, Thomas, 66; on town committee, 9; ensign, 99; wounded by Indians, 105, 124.
Bulkeley, Rev. Edward, 90; petitioner, 78; attorney for his brother, 82; succeeds his father, 21; new agreement of town with him, 25; criticisms of him, 31; spelling of the name, 41; his house-lot, 88; his certificate, 147.
> Grace, her embarkation, 1; sells estate to Wheelers, 89; Buss's deed to her, 94; her dispute with town about mill privilege, 96.
> Rev. John, returns to England, 37.
> Rev. Peter, his embarkation, 1; his English home, 3; founder of Concord, 1; chosen teacher, 2, 3; name, how spelled, 42; treaty with Indians at his house, 12, 14, 16; sole pastor, 24; his salary, ib.; writes petition in Martin's case, 28; his conduct in Jones matter, 36; death and burial, 41, 43; character and position, 42-45; his letters, 42, 43; his attitude towards the Indians, 100; his rate, 76; his farm, 81; buys estate of Hayward, 85; his dwelling-place, 68, 86, 89, 131; his library, 128; grants to, 94; builds town mill, 94; covenant about mill privilege, 96.
> Peter, Esquire, son of Rev. Edward, 90; chosen to assist in seating the meeting-house, 26; on committee to treat with the Bloods, 64; name, how spelled, 41; his house-lot, 86, 91; military offices, 122, 126; his position and services, 90, 91; his interest in the Iron Works, 136; his widow's petition for confirmation of title, 150.
> Peter, of London, apothecary, 82.
> Rebecca, petitions for confirmation of title, 150.

Bulkeley's Farm, 82.
Burgess, Thomas, 89; his house-lot, 86.
Burial-Hill, The, 86, 97.
Burying-Grounds, 88; their age, 97, 98; fencing them, 98, 99.
Buss, Joseph, 124.
> Nathaniel, 146.
> William, 3, 28, 73; keeps ordinary but declines to sell liquor, 138, 139; chirurgeon, 30; his house-lot, 88, 31; overseer, 76; his deed to Grace Bulkeley, 94; keeps mill, 95; ensign, 125; his petition, 126; lieutenant, 127.

Buttrick, Joseph, killed by Indians, 105.
> William, his embarkation, 1; his English home, 3; opposes division of highways, 70; his testimony, 13, 17; his house-lot, 88; released from training, 121.

CAATO, alias Goodmans, 16; sells Sudbury five miles, 16.
Cade, Jack, 47.
Cambridge, 15, 84, 108; grant to, 50.
    Farms, road to, 80.
Carlisle, 54, 62, 65; District of, 8; incorporated, 8.
Carts, impressment of, 5.
Casumpal } James and Sarah, 59, 60.
Casumpat
Catechizing of children, &c., 24, 129.
Cattle, how herded and pastured, 19, 20, 103; commons for, 55; branding of, 103; dry, pasturing of, 56.
Cedar Swamp, 9.
Chambers, Charles, 82.
Charities, early, 133, 134.
Charlestown, 15, 41; road to, 80.
Charter, of the Colony, its dissolution, 90; proceedings against, 147, 148; of the Province, 148.
Chelmsford laid out, 51, 54, 55, 59, 62, 66, 113, 124; bridge, 77.
Church, The, organization of, 3, 22, 23; not transplanted, 2; affairs of, how conducted, 26; petition of, 28, 29; advised by Boston elders, 35; how affected by Mr. Jones's removal, 36; members of, 147.
Clark, William, buys land, 94.
Clerk of the Writs, 21.
Cliffs, The, 67.
Colburn house-lot, 81, 85.
Commissioners for the Colonies, their order, 2; for improving meadows, 31; to end small matters, 20.
Common, The, line of, 94; encroached upon by mill-pond, 92.
Commons, habitations privileged with, to be recorded, 19; votes of town about, 55; not to be overcharged, 20; to be used for repair of mill damage, 94, 97; cow, defined, 68; to be allowed to poor men, 134.
Comy, Daniel, killed by Indians, 105.
Concord, first inland plantation, 50; name of, 5; immunity from public charges, 5, 37; Old, map of, 5-10, 32; Wood's plan of, 7; map of, by Hales, 7; petition for reduction of rates, 38, 39; enlargement of, 50, 52; return of land by, 51; River, 8, 9, 10, 61, 71; abatement of falls in river, 33; sale of weir, &c., at, 16; fire in, 34; population and resources, 37, 138; rates assessed upon, 37; rates reduced, 40; removal from, prohibited, 40; petitions for land, 52, 53; old bounds of, 7-10, 32, 59; trouble with the Bloods about taxes, 63; makes agreement with them, 64, 65; controversy with Billerica and the Bloods, 65, 66; old records of, 66; meeting of, about second divisions, 68; divided

into quarters, 68; object of the division, 69; relieved in part from expense of bridges, 77, 79; description of, in 1666, 84; men killed by Indians, 105; keeps day of thanksgiving, 113; military preparations at, 114; fined for want of watch-house, stocks, &c., 117; magazine at, 114, 119; its military company to be exercised, 120; its garrison-houses, 123; ordered to choose a constable in place of Wm. Buss, 127; foot-company of, divided, 128; education in, 128–133; subscribes for Harvard College, 130; gift to, from Capt. Timothy Wheeler, 129, 131; early charities of, 133, 134; amusements in, 140; its action at the time of the Andros Revolution, 151; only town to declare for war, 152.

Concord Village. (See New Grant.)
Conoway, Peter and Sarah, 59, 60, 61.
Constable, office of, 19.
Cornfields to be fenced, 19.
Coslin } William, 35.
Costin }
Cotton, John, exchanges cows with town, 26.
    Rev. John, 23.
Court-house, building of, 92, 93.
Courts, where held, 92.
Cowdrey, William, 101.
Cranefield, 19, 67, 68.
Curry, David, killed by Indians, 105.
Curtis, Ephraim, 111, 113.

DAKIN, John, his dwelling-place, 85.
    Joseph, fences burying-places, 99.
    Thomas, 73; sells estate to Heywood, 85; his dwelling-place, *ib.*
Dane, Daniel, 146; buys farm with Goble, 83.
    Joseph, his dwelling-place, 87.
    Thomas, 73; embarks with Mrs. Bulkeley, 1; his English home, 3; his house lot, 71, 74, 86, 93, 97.
Danforth, Jonathan, his plans, 6; surveys Billerica line, 9; on committee to settle mill dispute, 97.
Davis, Samuel, 146; Junior, 9.
    Simon, 146; his dwelling-place, 89; makes no return of land, 89; lieutenant, 127, 147; at Brookfield, 110, 111.
Davy, 103.
Deaths, record of, 21.
Dedham, meeting-house at, 22; removal from, prohibited, 40.
Deer Island, Indians removed to, 115, 117.
Depositions about Indian purchase, 12–15.
Deputies, residence of, 20.

Divisions, First and Second, 18, 67; how made, 68, 69, 74; not to hinder highways, 69.
Doggett, Thomas, 35.
Dongye Hole, 72, 73.
Dorchester, settlement of, 2.
Draper, Goody, convicted, 103.
    Roger, 38.
Dublet, Thomas, convicted, 102.
Dudley, Francis, his dwelling-place, 85.
    Gov. Joseph, 90; his appointment, 148.
    Gov. Thomas, his farm, 61.
Dunsdell, 81.
D'Urfey, Thomas, quoted, 47.
Dwellings, first, situation of, 18.

EAMES family, massacre of, 116.
"East End," 75, 76.
"East Quarter Line," 72.
Edmonds, Joshua, 70, 73.
    Walter, 40.
Education, 128–133.
Egg Rock, 71.
Eliot, Rev. John, 102, 115.
Elmbrook Meadow, 67.
Endicott, Gov. John, 29, 45.
Enfield, 24.
Enlargement of bounds. (See New Grant.)
Estabrook, Rev. Joseph, settled as colleague, 24; his burial-place, 43; compared with Mr. Edward Bulkeley, 31.
Evarts, John, 35.

FAIRFIELD, 35.
Fairhaven, 73, 83, 103; way to, 81; mining operations at, 137.
Farm-houses, 21.
Farrar, Jacob, killed by Indians, 105.
    Stephen, 124.
Farwell, Henry, 28, 68, 71.
    John, his house-lot, 86.
Fidelity, oath of, substituted for freeman's oath, 145; those taking it to be recorded, 20.
Fields, Great Common, 81, 83.
Fifty-Acre Meadow, 81.
Fiske, John, at Brookfield, 110.

Flagg, Eleazer, 147; constable, 63; granted land for tan-pits, 93, 94; his house, 131; sells land to Clark, 94.
Fletcher, Francis, 22; his house-lot, 86.
 Hezekiah, 131.
 Joseph, 22, 82.
 Samuel, 82, 146.
 William, his house-lot, 86.
Flint's Farm, description of, 82; way to, 81.
 Pond, 72, 73, 82; ditch from, 68, 95.
Flint, John, 20, 26, 57, 59; town clerk, 66; his house-lot, 88; lieutenant, 125.
 Thomas, 2, 3; his character and services, 45, 46; his death, 41; his farm, 82; assists Indians, 101.
Fort Bridge, 79.
Founell, John, 97.
Fox, Eliphalet, selectman, 146; his house-lot, 86.
 Thomas, 28, 29.
Fox's Bridge, 79.
Freemen, how admitted, 145–147.
French, Joseph, 9, 147; selectman, 152.
Frizzell, William, 85; released from training, 121.
Frontier Towns, removal from, prohibited, 40; troop for, 122.
Fuller, William, fined, 94.
Fur-trade, company for, 17.

GARFIELD, Benjamin and Thomas, 32.
Garrison-houses, their erection and situation, 123.
Goble, Thomas, 146; buys farm with Dane, 83.
Gomps, 53.
"Goodman" and "Goodwife," how applied, 27.
Goodmans, 16..
Goodman's Hill, 16.
Gookin, Gen. Daniel, 46; friend of the Indians, 102, 115; his report about them, 117; his report about the Concord military company, 127.
Goose Pond, 68, 72.
Grammar School, 128.
Grant, First, 5; map of, 5–10; how laid out, 7, 17; its bounds, 7; description of, 17; excess in, as laid out, 11; New, 50–61.
Graves, John, 28.
Great Common Fields, 81.
Great James Natocotos, 53.
Great Meadow, 81, 83.
Griffin, Richard, 28, 40, 45.

Groton, road to, 81; town destroyed by Indians, 41; people seek refuge in Concord, 104.

HABITATIONS privileged with commons, record of, 19.
Hales, John G., his survey and map, 7.
Half-way Brook, 79.
Halsted, William, his gift to the town, 133.
Hartford, founders of, 37.
Hartwell, John, 146; his house-lot, 87.
    Samuel, 147.
    William, 20, 78, 123; his house-lot, 87; overseer, 76.
Harvard College, early graduates, 37; aid to, 130.
Harwood, Nathaniel, 146.
Hayward, George, 52, 71, 73, 74, 124; on committee to divide highways, &c., 70; sells estate to Mr. Bulkeley, 85; overseer, 76; his land, 85; death, *ib.*; builds mills, 95; killed by Indians, 105.
    John, 127, 146, 147.
    Joseph, 120.
Heald, Major Benj. F., 8.
    Dorothy, her house-lot, 88.
    John, 3; his house-lot, 88; lieutenant, 150.
Heywood, John, buys estate of Dakin, 85, 88; constable's return, 118; keeps ordinary, 139, 140.
Henry, Indian, convicted, 103.
Higginson, Rev. Francis, 33.
Highways, not hindered by second division, 69; division of, 69, 74, 75; to be maintained by Quarters, 75; defined, 75, 79-81; north of Burying-Ground on Main Street, 88; same discontinued, 98.
Hinchman, Thomas, 122; captain of troop, 125; petitions for confirmation of title, 150.
Hingham, meeting-house at, 92.
Hoar, John, 26, 89; prosecution of, 30, 31; his estate, 89; exchanges lands with Wright, 89; takes charge of Indians, 115-117; his petition, 117.
Hog-pen, Old, 70, 81.
Hog-pens, 103.
Hog-pen Walk, 68, 70.
Hooker, Rev. Thomas, 37.
Horsmonden, 1.
Hosmer, James, 66, 73; his embarkation, 2; English home, 3; member of the church, 28; overseer, 76; his house-lot and farm, 84, 85; selectman, 139.
    James, Junior, his farm, 85; killed by Indians, *ib.*, 105.
    Capt. Stephen, 6, 11, 83, 133.

INDEX. 163

Hosmer, Stephen, selectman, 146, 152; buys "Brook-Meadow," 91.
Hough, Atherton, grant to, 61.
    Mrs., 59.
House-lots, how laid out, 18, 67; location of, 81–89.
Houses, early, description of, 21; their situation, 37; not to be built more than half a mile from meeting-house, except, 21.
How, Samuel, 124, 147.
Howe, John, 66.
Hubbard, Jonathan, 146.
Hunt, John, 83.
    Samuel, 117; his house-lot, 88.
    William, 3, 40; buys land of Mr. Bulkeley, 86.
    Nehemiah, 20, 146; his dwelling-place, 86.
Hutchinson, Capt. Edward, his expedition, 108.

INDIANS, purchase from, 3, 12–16; destroy Groton, 41; their paths one foot broad, 4, 79; treatment of them by colonists, 100–104; sale of liquor to them, 101; their claim to New Grant extinguished, 52, 56–60; of Musketaquid, 12; land reserved for, 53; their claim to Blood's Farms extinguished, 61; their habits and occupations, 101; value of their testimony, 103; sales of pork by, 104; war with, under Philip, 104–119; Concord men killed and wounded by, 105; the attack on the Shepards, 106; fight with, at Brookfield, 108–113; "Praying" suspected, 114; ordered to Deer Island and Concord, 115, 124; taken away by Mosley, 116, 117.
Ingolds, Ebenezer, 60.
Inheritance, law of, 47.
Iron Works, 19, 91; authorized in Concord, 135; land of, ib., 136; clerk of, 140.

JAYS, destruction of, 19.
Jehoiakin, his testimony, 13, 15, 16.
Jenckes, Joseph, 136.
Jethro, his testimony, 14, 16.
John Tahatowon, 53.
John Thomas, 53, 58, 60.
Johnson, Capt. Edward, quoted, 3, 4, 18.
Jones, Ephraim, 136; buys Wright Tavern lot, 92.
    Rev. John, 14, 15, 24, 28; chosen pastor, 23; his removal to Connecticut, 35, 39.
    John, 52, 53, 146; his house-lot, 88.
    Samuel, 136; clerk of the bona, 127.

Joseph, 110.
Josiah, 103.
Judson, Grace, 22.
    Jeremiah, Joseph, and Joshua, 22.
    William, his lot, 22.

KENT, County of, 2, 3; shield and motto of, 47; its influence in Middlesex, 46–48, 152.
King Philip's War, 104.
Knight, Jonathan, 136.

LAMSON, Elizabeth, 143.
    Widow, 143.
Lancaster, 7, 41; road, 74, 78, 85; people seek refuge in Concord, 104.
Land, character of, 33, 34, 38, 39, 50; petition for, by Wheeler and others, 38, 49; town's petition for, 50; waste, how rated, 64; common and undivided, 83; report about, 83; flowed by millpond, 96; titles declared void, 149; tenure of, 150; division of, 18; grants of, how recorded, 84; transcripts of, 84; lease of, 19; to be truly brought in, 20; deficiency in, made up, 71, 83.
Law, John, tenant of town, 55; rent due from him, 19, 20.
    Stephen, tenant of town, 55.
Lechford, Thomas, quoted, 24.
Lee, Joseph, 83.
Leihtenegger, Augustus, works mine at Fairhaven, 137.
Lettin, Richard, 38.
Lexington, 48; line of, on Bedford, 10.
Lincoln, 32; bounds of, in part, 10.
Liquor, sale of, 101, 138–140.
Littleton, 54.
Lovewell's Fight, 113.

MANTATUCKET, 14.
Marlborough, 112; road, 80.
Marriages, record of, 21; how contracted, 141–143.
Marshall, Capt. Thomas, buys estate of Willard, 41; sells to Woodis, 85.
Martin, Ambrose, prosecution of, 26–30; petition of the church in his favor, 28; his house and land sold, 29.
Mashoba, 52. (See Nashoba.)
Mason, Capt. Hugh, 105.
Massachusetts Bay, Colony of, 104; the Province, 148.
Mather, Rev. Cotton, 27, 140; quoted, 24.

INDEX. 165

Meadow, Great, 67; town, 67, 68, 72; reserved for minister, 70.
Meadows, wetness of, 33, 34, 38, 39; to be protected from animals, 19; division of, 67.
Meeting House, first, timber for, 22; location of, 21, 22, 97; second, building of, 19, 91; seating of, 26; description and use of, 92, 93; weather-vane on, 93.
" Meeting-house Frame, The," 22.
Meeting-house Green, 94.
Merchant Thomas, 14, 15, 53.
Meriam, George, 68, 71, 73; his house-lot, 87.
    John, 147; his house-lot, 87.
    Joseph, his gift to the town, 20; his grave-stone, 97.
    Robert, 28, 68, 71, 73; selectman, 139; his gift to the town, 134; deacon, 26; his house-lot, 87; on committee to divide highways, &c., 70,
    Samuel, 147.
Middlebrook, Joseph, 35, 40.
Middlesex County, map of, 7; its population, 46, 48; bridges, 77.
Miles, John, 20, 73; his house-lot, 88.
Mill, town, 89, 94–97, 131; houses, 21.
Mill-pond, how formed, 95; encroaches upon Common, 92.
" Mill-dam, The," 95.
Mill Brook, 18, 78; division line between Quarters, 71, 72; bridges over, 79; house-lots laid out to, 86; pond formed by, 95.
Military preparations at Concord, 114; draft ordered, 119; company, beginning of, 120; duty, persons subject to, *ib.*; exemptions, 121; officers, 121–127; arms, 121; offices and titles, how esteemed, 125; companies reorganized, 125, 127; foot company, divided, 128; despatched to Boston, 150.
Militia, committee of, 123; of Concord, their request, 124.
Mine Hill, 137.
Mine House, 137.
Mining operations, 135–137.
Ministerial wood-lot, 131.
Ministers, rates for, 19; support of, 35; their ordination, 23; wood for, 25; method of settling, 26; their numbers and character, 36, 37.
Minott, James, 146; keeps the mill, 95, 131; captain, 127.
    Rebecca, 95, 131.
Mitchell, Jonathan, 3, 35.
Mosley, Captain, removes Indians, 116, 117.
" Mr. and Mrs.," how applied, 27.
Muckquamack, Peter, 57.
Musketaquid, 5; meaning of name, 71; settlement at, 1; River, 67, 71; name changed to Concord, 5.

Muttunkatucka, 13.
Mystic Bridge, 77.

NAGOG Pond, 55.
Naanonsquaw, 58, 60.
Naaruhpanit, 57, 59.
Narragansett Fort, fight at, 105.
Nashoba Plantation, 14, 51, 55, 59, 105, 106; line of, 54; deserted, 117.
    Brook, 55.
    Indians, removal of, 115-117; their return, 117.
Nasquaw, John, 50, 60.
Natanquaticke, 16.
Natick, 14, 57; Indians, 115.
Natocotos, Great James, 53.
Nattatawants, grant to, 51; sells land, 62.
Nashawtuck, 14, 67, 81; bridge near, 69, 78.
Neepanaum, Mary, 57.
New Grant, The, plan of, 6; petition and orders for, 50-53; for feeding, 52, 103; Indian claim to, 52; laid out by Beers and Noyes, 53, 54; to be a free common, &c., 55; deeds of land included in, 56-60; bounds of, 65.
Nimrod, 14, 15.
Nine-Acre Corner, 81, 137.
Nipmuck Country, 108.
North River, bridges over, 19, 71.
North Quarter, roads in, 81. (See Quarters.)
Notawquatuckquaw, 14, 15.
Nowell, Increase, grant to, 61, 65.
Noyes, Thomas, surveyor, 53, 54.
Nssquan, 53.
Nuttankatucka, 13.

ODELL, village, 1, 42.
Odell, William, 35.
Oldmans, 16.
Ordinaries, 138-141.
Overseers of the Quarters, 75, 76.

PARKER, Moses, 58.
Pellet, Daniel, 99, 147.
    Mary, 144.

Pellet, Thomas, 147; his dwelling-place, 87; assisted by the town, 133; loses his dinner, 144.
Pennsylvania, grants in, how laid out, 11.
Persons, undesirable, not to be entertained, 20.
Phips, Sir William, Governor, 148.
Pittamey, Andrew, 60.
Plans of towns, 6.
Plymouth, settlement at, 2.
Pompant, 53.
Ponkapog Indians, 115.
Poor, support of, 133, 134; silent, 143.
Pork, sale of, regulated, 104.
Potter, Judah, 116.
    Luke, 28, 71, 73; deacon, 26; his house-lot, 73, 86.
    Samuel, killed by Indians, 105.
Potter's Bridge, 79.
    Lane, 86.
Pound, town, 93, 94.
Power, Mary, 144.
Pratt, Thomas, 82.
Prescott, Jonathan, 79; his dwelling-place, 98; lieutenant, 147; chirurgeon, 30; grant of land to, 98.
Prout, Ebenezer, builds mill, 95; clerk, 128, 146, 147, 151; takes poor child as apprentice, 132; signs order for removal of Andros to the Castle, 151.
    Timothy, 82.
Prout's Farm, 82.
    Folly, 95.
Public Houses, 138–140.

QUABAUG, 108.
Quarters, division of town into, 68; limits of, 71–74; South or West, 70; its limits, 71, 72; division of wood in, 72; East, its limits, 71, 72; North, its limits, 71; assignment to them of highways and bridges, 74, 75; to hold town harmless from damage for defective ways, &c., 75; overseers of, 75, 76; records of, 84.

RAINER, Samuel, 29.
Rates, minister, 19, 25, 61; public, how payable, 37, 40; for highways, 75, 76.
Read, Dr. Philip, 27; prosecution of, 30–32.
Rice, Peter, 144.

Rice, Richard, 31, 71; his testimony, 13, 17; his dwelling-place, 71, 73, 85, 87.
    Timothy, 124, 146.
Richardson, James, 110.
Ripley, Dr. Ezra, quoted, 43.
River, how crossed, 78.
Robinson, Rev. John, 2.
" Rocks, The," way to, 81.
Rocky Hill, 72.
Rogers, John, 29.
Roper, Ephraim, 82.
Ross, Daniel, 134.
Russell, James, owns Iron Works, 136.
Rutter, Jabesh, 112.

SAMPSON, 110.
Saw-mills, 22, 95.
Schools and school-houses, 128–133.
School-master, want of, 129.
School-house lot, 131.
Scotchford, John, 73; his house-lot, 88.
    Lane, 128.
Scotland, 81.
Scudder, H. E., quoted, 27.
Selectmen, instructions to, 19, 20; their powers and duties, 20; to impose fines, 76; to superintend erection of fortifications, 123; their return of non-freemen, 146.
Settlers, early, character of, 2, 46–48; their former homes, 3; journey to Musketaquid, 3, 4; hardships suffered, 33–41; their educational attainments, 132.
Sewall, Samuel, 150.
Shamberry, Joseph, 60, 61.
Shattuck, Lemuel, his History, 7; his papers, 6, 28, 43.
Shawshine, grant to, 51; River, 8, 9; Corner, 10, 68, 81; road to, 137.
Sheep, &c., damage by, 19.
Shepard, Abraham, 106, 107.
    Isaac, killed by Indians, 105–107, 112; his estate, 107.
    Jacob, 106, 107.
    John, 53, 146.
    Mary, captured by Indians, 106, 107, 112, 116.
    Ralph, buys Nashoba Farm, 55.
Short Swamp, 73.
Skinner, Thomas, 82.

Smedly, Baptist, his dwelling-place, 88; his daughter, 107; his death and estate, 112.
 James, 144, 146; his house-lot, 87.
 John, 26, 40, 64, 144; on committee to divide highways, &c., 70; overseer, 76; his house-lot, 88; on committee to build meeting-house, 91; released from training, 121; his report about schools, 129.
 Samuel, killed by Indians, 112; his estate, *ib.*
Soldiers, impressment of, 124. (See Military.)
Solomon Thomas, 59, 60.
South Field, 67.
 River, 73; bridge over, 69, 74; road to, 88.
Speen, John and Sarah, 57, 58.
 James and Elizabeth, 57, 58.
Spelling, irregular habits of, 132.
Spencer, William, 14, 15; his land in Concord, 15.
Spencer Brook, 15, 86, 95.
Squaw Sachem, 13–16.
Squaws, escape of, 118.
Stannup, Hannah, 144.
Stockadoes, line of, ordered, 114.
Stocks, 117.
Stoughton, Gov. William, 90.
Stow, Nathaniel, 146; his house-lot, 86.
 Thomas, 70; his second division, 82.
Stow, town of, 57, 59.
Subsidy-men, departure of, forbidden, 2.
Sudbury, 50, 57, 113; line of, 10; ways, 75, 79; meeting-house, 98; petition about meadows, 31; removal from, forbidden, 40; fight at, with Indians, 85, 105.
Swamp Bridge, 79.
Swanscombe, 47, 48.
Swine, damage by, 19; how herded, 103; how marked and sold, 104.

TAHATOWAN, 13–16.
 John, 53.
Tally, Thomas, banished, 112.
Tar-kiln Brook, 137.
Tasattawan, 59.
Tasunsquaw, 58, 60.
Taylor, Abraham, 9, 117.
 John, 124.
 William, his house-lot, 87.
Taxes. (See Rates.)

Temple, Abraham, 105, 124, 146.
    Isaac, 146.
    Richard, 15, 146; his dwelling-place, 85; builds saw-mill, 95.
Thomas, John, 53, 58, 60.
    Solomon, 59, 60.
Titles, significance of, 27.
Tompkins, John, 35.
Townsmen, 19, 69. (See Selectmen.)
Town, officers of, 19; clerk, 21; bell, 92; house, 93; cow, 26, 133, 134; pound, 93; watch-house, 117; mill, 94-97; meadow, 67, 68, 72; record books, 84; meetings, 92; library, 128.
Training-field, 92.
Training-place, 71, 75.
Transcripts of lands, 84.
Troop of horse, 108, 122.
Turney, Benjamin, 35.
Twenty score, 83.

USHER, Herman and Hezekiah, engage in mining operations at Fairhaven, 137.

VANE, Gov. Henry, 23.
Virginia, 81.

WABAN, 14, 15, 58.
    Thomas, 59, 60.
Wabatut, 53.
Walden Pond, 12, 72, 79, 80.
Walling, H. F., his maps of county and town, 7.
Wamesit, 57.
Wappacowet, 15.
Waste water, The, 92.
Watch-house, situation of, 117.
Watertown, 3, 50, 114; controversy with, about bounds, 12; bounds of, 32; road, 79, 80; corner, 81; company, 105.
Wayland, line of, 10.
Ways, private, 81. (See Highways.)
Webb, Cowet, 16.
Weston, bounds of, 32.
Wheat, John, 125.
    Moses, 29; his house-lot, 86.
    Samuel, 147.

Wheeler, Ephraim, 35, 38.
 Ensign, 70, 71, 73.
 George, 28, 40, 52, 66, 73, 78; selectman, 139; on committee to divide highways, &c., 70; overseer, 76; his house-lot, 87; joint-owner with Capt. Timothy, 89; sells land to Prescott, 98.
 John, 124, 146, 147; constable, 63; his house-lot, 87; sergeant, 99.
 Joseph, 28, 40, 52, 53, 90, 124; grant to, 55; his house-lot, 87; on committee to build meeting-house, 91.
 Joshua, 79, 146; his house-lot, 87.
 Josiah, killed by Indians, 105.
 Obadiah, 73, 146; his dwelling-place, 75, 85.
 Samuel, Jr., 58.
 Sergeant, 68.
 Thomas, Senior, his house-lot, 86.
 Thomas, 20, 28, 35; selectman, 146, 152; petitioner, 38, 49; Junior, 38, 110, 113.
 Capt. Thomas, 125; takes lease from town, 19, 55. 56, 103; commands troop, 122; his "Narrative," 108; accompanies Capt. Hutchinson, 108-113; his certificate to the Indians, 110; his return celebrated, 113.
 Timothy, 147; petitioner, 38, 40, 52, 78; overseer, 76.
 Capt. Timothy, 26; his house, 14; his estate, 89; negotiates with Indians, 57, 59; on committee to build meeting-house, 91; keeps mill, 95; authorized to impress gunsmith, 114; captain of foot company, 122, 125; his return of soldiers impressed, 124, 125; his gift to the town, 129, 131.
 Rebecca, 90.
 William, 6, 73.
Wiggin, John and Mary, 90.
Wigly, Edmund, his dwelling-place, 85.
Willard, Simon, 28, 73; founder of Concord, 1; his English home, 3; trades with Indians, ib., 17; lays out the township, 5, 12, 17; commands foot company, 120, 122; conducts negotiations with Indians about lands, 14, 15, 61; on valuing committee, 37; excused from attendance on court, 41; his removal to Lancaster, ib.; commissioner, 45; his character and services, 43, 44; his farms, 51, 59, 65, 66, 136; assists Indians, 101, 115; on highway committee, 70; on committee to settle mill dispute, 97; relieves Wheeler at Brookfield, 112.
Winnetow, Dorothy, 57, 58.
Winnippin, 62.
Winthrop, Gov. John, 23; his farm, 61.
Woburn Corner, 10.
 Road, 80.
Wompachowet, 14.

Wood, Abraham, 146.
    Ephraim, surveys town, 7.
    John, 124, 146.
    Michael, 71, 74; his dwelling-place, 85; clerk of the Iron Works, 140.
    William, 3, 37, 40, 73.
Woodis, Henry, 14, 26, 57, 59, 64, 70, 78, 122; his second division, 82; his dwelling-place, 85.
Woodis's Rock, 83.
Woolley, Christopher, 89; his dwelling-place, 87.
    Joseph, 60.
    Thomas, 125.
Wormwood, Joseph, 136.
Wright, Edward, 89, 143; his house-lot, 86; exchanges land with Hoar, 89; of Castle Brownick, 90; builds saw-mill, 95.
    Francis, 90.
    Peter, his marriage contract, 143; his gift to the town, *ib.*
    Samuel, 136, 143.

YOUNG, Henry, killed by Indians, 113.

www.ingramcontent.com/pod-product-compliance
Lightning Source LLC
Chambersburg PA
CBHW020844160426
43192CB00007B/775